The Biology of Twinning in Man

M. G. Bulmer

Lecturer in Biomathematics in the University of Oxford

WITHDRAWN

The Biology of
Twinning in Man

CLARENDON PRESS · OXFORD

1970

Oxford University Press, Ely House, London W.1

GLASGOW NEW YORK TORONTO MELBOURNE WELLINGTON
CAPE TOWN SALISBURY IBADAN NAIROBI DAR ES SALAAM LUSAKA ADDIS ABABA
BOMBAY CALCUTTA MADRAS KARACHI LAHORE DACCA
KUALA LUMPUR SINGAPORE HONG KONG TOKYO

MADE IN GREAT BRITAIN AT
THE PITMAN PRESS, BATH

Contents

List of Figures

List of Tables

1 The Two Types of Twins

SOME twins resemble each other so closely that it is difficult to distinguish between them. This fact has been recognized since antiquity, and the confusion of twins has been a favourite theme of comic dramatists since the *Menaechmi* of Plautus (*c.* 200 B.C.) which was the main source of Shakespeare's *Comedy of Errors.* Other twins can be easily distinguished, like Jacob and Esau, whose story is told in the Bible (*Genesis* 25–27) and who differed in temperament ('And Esau was a cunning hunter, a man of the field; and Jacob was a plain man, dwelling in tents'), in appearance ('Behold, Esau my brother is a hairy man, and I am a smooth man'), and in speech ('The voice is Jacob's voice, but the hands are the hands of Esau').

The accepted explanation of these facts is that there are two types of twins, the first derived from the division of a single zygote (fertilized ovum) at some stage in the development of the embryo after fertilization, and the second from the independent release and subsequent fertilization of two ova. Twins of the first type will be genetically identical, while those of the second type will be no more alike genetically than ordinary brothers and sisters. The two types of twins are in consequence often known as identical and fraternal twins, but in scientific usage they are more often called monozygotic and dizygotic twins to indicate their origin from a single zygote or from two zygotes; the latter usage will be adopted in this book.

The existence of these two types of twins has been taken as

common knowledge among scientists for a century (Price 1950, Corner 1955). However, it has also been suggested that there may be a third type of twin derived from the fertilization of two ova which have not been independently released but have been formed by the division of a single ovum before fertilization; such twins would usually be intermediate between monozygotic and dizygotic twins in their degree of genetic similarity. In this chapter we shall first consider the evidence which demonstrates the existence of monozygotic twins, and we shall then discuss whether all other twins are dizygotic or whether there is also a third type of twin intermediate between monozygotic and dizygotic twins.

Evidence of monozygotic twinning in man

Proof of the existence of monozygotic twins rests on several lines of evidence, both genetic and anatomical, none of which is completely conclusive by itself but which, taken together, show beyond all doubt that many human twins are monozygotic.

Indirect evidence of monozygotic twinning is provided by the fact that many twins are found at birth to have been enclosed in a single chorionic membrane. This condition is most easily explained by supposing that the twins arose by division of the embryo at some stage in development after the formation of the chorion; it will be discussed fully in the next chapter. Additional evidence is provided by the occurrence of conjoined (Siamese) twins which probably arise by incomplete division of the embryo. Embryologists have also found several early twin embryos which provide direct proof that human twins may arise from a single ovum; an excellent review has been written by Corner (1955). But the most extensive and most convincing evidence of the existence of monozygotic twins is genetic rather than anatomical.

The simplest piece of genetic evidence is provided by the sex combinations of twins. The sex of an embryo is determined by whether the ovum is fertilized by a spermatozoon carrying a female-determining X chromosome or a male-determining Y

chromosome. These two types of spermatozoa occur with almost equal frequency, which is the reason why nearly equal numbers of boys and girls are born. (In fact there is a slight excess of boys, but it is too small to affect the argument.) It follows that monozygotic twins must always be of the same sex, while twins of any other type, for which two separate spermatozoa are responsible, are equally likely to be of the same sex or of different sexes. In fact more like-sexed than unlike-sexed twins are born. For example, the Registrar-General's Statistical Review of England and Wales for 1960 records that 9,086 pairs of twins were born in that year, of whom 5,894 were like-sexed (either two boys or two girls) and 3,192 were unlike-sexed (one boy and one girl). The existence of the unlike-sexed twins shows immediately that not all twins are monozygotic. On the other hand, the preponderance of like-sexed twins can most easily be explained by postulating the existence of a number of monozygotic twins nearly equal to the excess of like-sexed over unlike-sexed twins. This excess is 2,702 or about thirty per cent of the total. Further-more, the total number of maternities in 1960 was 791,584, so that the relative frequency of monozygotic twins can be estimated as about 3·4 per thousand maternities. This method of estimating the frequency of monozygotic twins is known as Weinberg's method; it will be discussed more fully in Chapter 4.

After sex the most valuable genetic characters in the study of twins are the blood groups, since they are relatively easy to determine, they are under complete genetic control, and their mode of inheritance is well understood. One of the most exten-sive studies of the blood groups of twins was made by Cederlöf, Friberg, Jonsson and Kaij (1961) who sent a questionnaire to 200 pairs of like-sexed Swedish twins asking them, among other things, whether, when growing up, they were 'as like as two peas' or only of ordinary family likeness. In 72 cases both twins stated that they had been as like as two peas, and in 113 cases both twins stated that they were only of ordinary family likeness; the replies of the remaining 15 pairs were either inconsistent, ambiguous, or deficient. The authors then determined the ABO, MN, Rhesus, and haptoglobin groups of these twins, and also the Gm serum groups of those pairs who were alike in the other four groups. They found that 71 out of the 72 pairs who stated that they had been as like as two peas were alike in all five blood groups tested, while of the 113 pairs of ordinary family likeness only 11 were alike in all five groups. The data are set out in Table 1.1.

Table 1.1. Blood groups and self-assessment of similarity in like-sexed twins (Cederlöf *et al.* 1961)

	Alike in all five blood groups	Different in at least one group	Total
Both twins as like as two peas	71	1	72
Both twins only of ordinary family likeness	11	102	113
Inconsistent, ambiguous or deficient replies	6	9	15
Total	88	112	200

It will be shown in the Appendix to this chapter that the probability that a pair of dizygotic twins should be alike in all five of these blood groups is about five per cent. If twins of the postulated third type exist who are identical on their mother's side but not on their father's side the probability that they should be identical in these blood groups is about twenty-three per cent. The fact that all but one of the 72 pairs of twins who stated that they had been as like as two peas were also alike in their blood groups can only be explained by supposing that nearly all of them are monozygotic.

We can also make an approximate calculation of the total number of monozygotic twins in the group. It seems likely that all the 71 twins who regarded themselves as alike and who were also alike in their blood groups are really monozygotic; this is therefore the minimum number of monozygotic twins. On the other hand, the maximum number of twins who could be monozygotic is 88, although it is likely that a few of the twins with identical blood groups are dizygotic since five per cent of dizygotic twins are expected to have identical blood groups. We shall probably not be far wrong if we suppose that about 80 of these 200 like-sexed twins are monozygotic. Furthermore, if forty per cent of like-sexed twins are monozygotic then twenty-five per cent of all twins must be monozygotic, on the assumption that half the non-monozygotic twins are like-sexed. This figure is rather lower than that of thirty per cent estimated earlier from the distribution of sex types. The discrepancy can probably be explained by the high frequency of dizygotic twinning in Sweden before the war (Eriksson 1964). In addition, the data on sex types were obtained at birth while the present data include only adult twins. We should expect the percentage of monozygotic twins to be rather lower among adult twins than among twins at birth since, as we shall see in Chapter 3, mortality is higher in monozygotic than in dizygotic twins.

Further evidence of the existence of monzygotic twins is provided by skin grafting. Skin cannot normally be grafted from one person to another, although it can be grafted from one part to another of the same person. Experiments on inbred strains of mice have shown that the failure of grafts between individuals is due to the existence of a large number of genes called histo-compatability genes: a graft from one person to another is only possible if the host possesses the same genes as the donor, which is highly unlikely except in an inbred strain (Medawar 1957, Stern 1960). This theory predicts that skin grafts can be made between monozygotic twins since they are genetically identical. There is now considerable clinical evidence that skin can in fact be grafted between twins thought on other grounds to be monozygotic but not between non-identical twins (Rogers 1963). An interesting anecdote concerns a French soldier who received severe burns with extensive skin loss during the Second World War. A few days later the 'patient' was seen walking round the hospital apparently in the best of health. On enquiry he proved to be the identical twin of the real patient, for whom he was able to supply a successful skin graft (Converse and Duchet 1947).

A possible objection to the evidence based on blood groups and skin grafting must now be discussed. In unlike-sexed cattle twins the male twin is normal but the female twin is often a freemartin, possessing male as well as female sexual characters. In 1916, Lillie showed that the free-martin condition was due to anastomosis of the foetal circulations in cattle twins; the partial masculinization of the female twin is caused by male sex hormones secreted by the male twin passing into the circulation of the female twin (Lillie 1916, 1917). In 1945, Owen found that most cattle twins have the same blood groups even when they are obviously not identical, and he was able to show that their blood in some cases consisted of a mixture of two types of blood, presumably as a result of the shared foetal circulation. In 1951, Anderson, Billingham, Lampkin, and Medawar found, to their surprise, that skin could normally be grafted between cattle twins even when they were of different sex and so could not possibly be monozygotic; the explanation is that the shared circulation in early foetal life caused an acquired tolerance of each other's tissues. In cattle twins, therefore, neither identical blood groups nor the success of skin grafts are evidence of genetic identity, since they may both be consequences of a common foetal circulation. Might the same be true in man?

Several cases have been reported of blood group chimaerae in human twins, that is to say twins whose blood is composed of a mixture of two distinct types of blood, presumably through mixture of the foetal circulations (Race and Sanger 1968). Skin grafts can be made between such twins, even though they are of different sexes, but they are sexually normal, probably because foetal sex hormones play a smaller part in sexual differentiation in man than in cattle. The phenomenon is however very rare; thus Race and Sanger (1962) report that they tested, without finding a mixture, samples of blood from 118 pairs of non-identical twins, in 106 of whom it should have been possible to detect such a mixture if it had existed. In a statistical study it therefore seems safe to ignore the existence of such twins. Furthermore, mixture of the foetal circulations cannot explain why skin grafts should succeed and why the blood groups should nearly always be identical in twins who are highly similar in other respects, but why this should not be true in physically dissimilar twins. Finally, as we shall see in the next chapter, there is no anatomical evidence of the fusion of the foetal circulations in dichorial twins, except in a very few cases. It can be concluded that identity of blood groups and the success of skin grafts can only very rarely be explained as the result of fusion of the foetal circulations in man.

Further evidence of the existence of monozygotic twins is provided by other characters which are largely but not entirely under genetic control. A considerable quantity of information has been collected about correlations between twins for different physical characters and in many cases very high correlations have been found between twins thought on other grounds to be identical. The data strongly suggest that these characters are to a large extent genetically determined and that the 'identical' twins are in fact monozygotic. The argument is in some danger of circularity but it does provide confirmatory evidence of the existence of monozygotic twins. The subject will be considered more fully in Chapter 7.

The evidence for the existence of monozygotic twins is completed by the occurrence of such twins in other mammals. Weinberg's method based on the distribution of sex types has been applied to a very extensive series of births in cattle to show that about seven per cent of cattle twins are probably monozygotic and that the frequency of monozygotic twinning is about 1·3 per thousand pregnancies (Hancock 1954). Probable cases of monozygotic twinning have also been reported in sheep (Cohrs 1934, Henning 1937) and in pigs (Cohrs 1934). It seems likely that monozygotic twins occur rather rarely in most mammals, although they are very difficult to detect; but the exception that proves the rule is provided by two closely related species of armadillo in which monozygotic twinning is

2

the normal method of reproduction. The nine-banded armadillo of Texas and Central America (*Dasypus novemcinctus*) regularly produces monozygotic quadruplets, and the mulita armadillo of South America (*Dasypus hybridus*) produces normally either eight or nine offspring derived from a single ovum, although as many as twelve have been observed. The monozygotic method of reproduction in these two armadillos has been proved beyond doubt by direct embryological evidence as well as by the fact that members of the same litter are always of the same sex (Newman 1917).

In conclusion, there is overwhelming evidence that many human twins are derived from the division of the embryo at some stage in its development after fertilization and are in consequence genetically identical. In the European data so far considered such monozygotic twins form about thirty per cent of all twins, but we shall see in Chapter 4 that this percentage varies considerably in different races and under different circumstances; however, the absolute frequency of monozygotic twins is rather constant at about three and a half to four per thousand maternities. It seems likely that monozygotic twinning occurs with a similar frequency in other mammals, apart from the armadillos mentioned above, although the evidence is rather scanty.

Is there a third type of twin?

It is generally believed that all non-monozygotic twins are dizygotic, being derived from the independent release and subsequent fertilization of two ova and in consequence having the same genetic similarity as ordinary brothers and sisters. However, it has also been suggested that there may be a third type of twin caused by the fertilization of ova which have not been independently released but have developed from the same primary oocyte. This suggestion was first made by Danforth (1916) to explain why Thorndike (1905) had found a unimodal rather than a bimodal curve when he plotted the frequency distribution of the difference between twins in several physical characters. Fisher (1919) investigated the theoretical form of this distribution from a mathematical-statistical viewpoint and concluded that it was consistent with the hypothesis that *all* twins were of a third type identical on the mother's but not on the father's side; however, he withdrew this suggestion in 1925 when further evidence became available which did not confirm Thorndike's findings.

The existence of a third type of twin has also been used to explain why the tendency to twinning can be inherited through the father as well as the mother (Curtius 1928); it has been suggested that the spermatozoa may sometimes cause the ovum to divide before fertilization, perhaps through some mechanical or chemical influence, and that the tendency to produce such twins may thus be inherited through the father. However, as we shall see in Chapter 6, it is rather doutful whether the tendency to produce twins is in fact inherited through the father.

Before considering the genetic evidence bearing on this question we must explain the genetic consequences of the postulated third type of twinning. It is first necessary to describe briefly the maturation of the ovum. The primary oocyte is a large cell in the ovary which divides unequally during the first meiotic division into the secondary oocyte which contains nearly all the cytoplasm and a much smaller cell called the first polar body. The secondary oocyte again divides unequally during the second meiotic division into the ovum and a much smaller cell called the second polar body. The first polar body may also divide again to give two first polar bodies. This process is shown diagrammatically in Fig. 1.1. The ovum is released from the ovary as a secondary oocyte and the second meiotic division only occurs immediately before fertilization.

There are three ways in which a third type of twin might develop. Firstly, the primary oocyte might divide equally instead of unequally during the first meiotic division, giving rise to two secondary oocytes and so to two ova. Secondly, the secondary oocyte might divide equally during the second

meiotic division, so giving rise to two ova. Thirdly, the ovum
itself might divide before fertilization. Following the terminology
of Mijsberg (1957), twins derived from the fertilization by two
spermatozoa of ova which have arisen in these three ways will
be called primary oocytary, secondary oocytary and uniovular
dispermatic twins respectively.

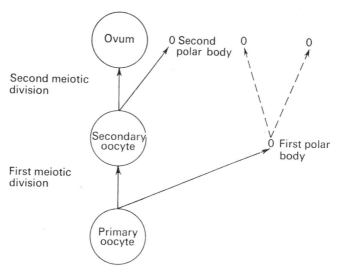

Fig. 1.1. Diagram of the maturation of the ovum.

We must now investigate the genetic consequnces of these
types of twinning. Uniovular dispermatic twins will be identical
on their mother's side only and will thus have half the genetic
variability of dizygotic twins since the ova from which they are
derived are genetically identical. The genetic similarity of ova
of the other two types depends on the mechanics of meiosis
which are illustrated in Fig. 1.2. The function of meiosis is to
reduce the number of chromosomes from the diploid number of
forty-six (in man) to the haploid number of twenty-three and
to ensure that the gametes receive one of each of the pairs of
homologous chromosomes; the diploid number is restored at
fertilization. The chromosome number is halved during the

first meiotic division, but the two chromatids of the chromosomes in the products of this division are not identical because crossing-over occurs between the chromatids of homologous chromosomes. The second meiotic division separates these two chromatids.

If crossing-over did not occur, the chromatids of the secondary

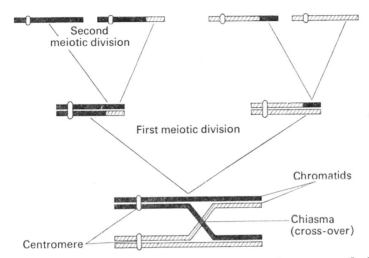

FIG. 1.2. The behaviour of a pair of homologous chromosomes during meoisis. The paternal chromosome is dark, the maternal chromosome light.

oocyte would be identical with each other but would be completely uncorrelated with the chromatids of the first polar body since they would be derived from different individuals, the woman's mother and father. In consequence, ova formed by an equal division of the secondary oocyte would be genetically identical, while ova formed by an equal division of the primary oocyte would be no more alike than ova chosen at random from different women. It is unlikely that crossing-over will occur near the centromere and so these results still hold good for genes located near the centromere. For genes located far from the centromere the probability of crossing-over will be $\frac{1}{2}$ and so both types of ova will be as alike as two separate ova from the same ovary which would give rise to dizygotic twins. The degree of likeness will be between these two extremes for genes located in an intermediate position. The exact degree of likeness for any particular gene will therefore depend on its distance from the centromere; but on the average, secondary oocytary ova will not be genetically identical but will be more alike than two independent ova from the same woman, while primary oocytary ova will be more alike than two ova from different women but less alike than two independent ova from the same woman. Hence, when these ova have been fertilized by different spermatozoa, secondary oocytary twins will be less alike than uniovular dispermatic twins but more alike than dizygotic twins, while primary oocytary twins will be less alike than dizygotic twins but more alike than two unrelated individuals. The different types of twins can therefore be ranked as follows in increasing order of their genetic similarity: primary oocytary, dizygotic, secondary oocytary, uniovular dispermatic, monozygotic.

There is some biological evidence for the occurrence of this third type of twinning. In flatworms, Francotte (1898) and Wilson (1925) have described the occurrence of giant first polar bodies which could be fertilized and develop into normal embryos and Gustafson (1946) has described the development of secondary oocytary twins in sea-urchins. The occurrence of giant first and second polar bodies has been described in several mammals (Austin 1961) and it seems likely that they are fertilizable, although it is uncertain whether they would develop into twins or into a single mosaic individual because of the presence of a thick membrane, the zona pellucida, round the mammalian ovum until the time of implantation. A remarkable recent development in human genetics has been the discovery of mosaic individuals with two genetically distinct cell lines which must have originated from different sperm. The first case described was a girl with a hazel left eye and a brown right eye; half her cells were found to be XY and half XX, and she also had two populations of red cells with different blood groups.

The genotypes of her parents showed that the differences in eye colour and blood groups must have come from her father's side and that two sperm must have been responsible for her engendering. Several other examples of dispermatic mosaicism have been reported and are reviewed by Race and Sanger (1968). In most cases it can be shown that the two types of cell present differ on the mother's as well as on the father's side and thus probably originate from the fertilization by two sperm of an ovum and of one of the polar bodies. It can be concluded that the mechanism postulated for the third type of twinning probably exists in man, but that it leads to mosaic individuals rather than twins; however, the possibility that twins may also be produced by these means cannot be excluded and we must now consider whether this possibility is supported by the facts available.

A considerable amount of evidence has been collected about the frequency with which non-identical twins are alike in different blood group systems. The data are summarized in Table 1.2, together with the expected degree of concordance

Table 1.2. Concordance for blood groups in non-identical twins

Blood group	Number of twins tested	Per cent concordant	Expected percentage	Reference
ABO	377	67	66	1, 2, 3
A_1A_2BO	397	59	62	4, 5, 6, 7, 8
MN	344	61	59	1, 8
MNS	132	48	48	5, 6
Rh (C, D, E, c)	131	50	50	5, 6
Rh (C, D, E, c, e)	100	56	49	8
P	70	74	78	5
Lewis	57	70	80	5
Duffy	70	67	74	5
Kell	70	86	91	5
Haptoglobin	100	62	61	8
Total	1848	62·0	62·4	

References: 1. Schiff and Verschuer (1933). 2. Gedda (1951), p. 486. 3. Osborne and de George (1957). 4. Sutton (1958). 5. Simmons, Graydon, Jakobowicz and Doig (1960). 6. Walsh and Kooptzoff (1955). 7. Race and Sanger (1962). 8. Cederlöf et al. (1961).

in dizygotic twins (see Appendix). There is good agreement between the observed and the expected proportions, so that the data do not reveal any evidence of the existence of a third type of twin. The presence of secondary oocytary or uniovular twins would be expected to increase the frequency of concordance, while the presence of primary oocytary twins would decrease this frequency. The data also fail to reveal any increase in the frequency of concordance for the ABO blood groups through incompatibility (Stern 1960).

A more sensitive test is provided by the distribution of the number of blood group differences in twins who have been tested for several systems. Table 1.3 shows this distribution for

Table 1.3. Distribution of the number of differences in four blood group systems in 197 pairs of like-sexed twins (Cederlöf et al. 1961)

Number of differences	0	1	2	3	4
Observed frequency	89	39	45	19	5
Expected frequency	—	40	44	21	4

the like-sexed twins in the study of Cederlöf, Friberg, Jonsson, and Kaij (1961) who were tested for the ABO, MN, Rhesus, and haptoglobin groups, together with the theoretical distribution among twins who differ in at least one group on the assumption that they are all dizygotic; Table 1.4 shows the same

Table 1.4. Distribution of the number of differences in three blood group systems in 99 pairs of non-identical twins (Simmons et al. 1960, Walsh and Kooptzoff 1955).

Number of differences	0	1	2	3
Observed frequency	19	33	34	13
Expected frequency	15	39	35	10

distribution for twins in two other studies who were tested for the ABO, MNS, and Rhesus systems and who were known to be non-identical on other grounds (through difference in sex, or some other blood group, or in physical appearance). In both cases there is good agreement with the theoretical distribution, so the data again fail to reveal any evidence of the existence of a third type of twin.

Another line of evidence of considerable value is provided by the occurrence of mongolism in twins. Mongolism is a congenital abnormality characterized by a variety of physical peculiarities, mostly due to retarded growth, and by severe mental deficiency. It is a relatively common condition; among Europeans about one baby in 700 is born a mongol, although the incidence in the adult population is much smaller because of its high mortality. It has been shown quite recently that mongolism is caused by the presence of an extra chromosome, probably chromosome 21. Most mongols have three of chromosome 21 instead of the usual pair. This condition is known as trisomy and is usually due to non-disjunction (i.e. failure of homologous chromosomes to separate) during meiosis, so that a gamete with two 21 chromosomes is produced which gives rise to a zygote with three such chromosomes; another gamete with no 21 chromosome must be formed at the same time but the zygote to which it gives rise with only a single 21 chromosome is probably inviable. Non-disjunction may occur at either the first or the second meiotic division. A less common type of mongolism is caused by the attachment of an extra 21 chromosome to one of the other chromosomes by translocation. The correlation of mongolism with maternal age and studies on its familial incidence indicate that the chromosomal abnormality usually occurs in the ovum rather than in the sperm (Penrose 1963).

Monozygotic twins must be concordant for mongolism unless, as happens rarely, the chromosomal abnormality occurs after fertilization. Concordant dizygotic twins, on the other hand, require two separate chromosomal abnormalities and will therefore be rare. If these abnormalities occurred independently the ratio of concordant to discordant dizygotic twins should be about half the frequency of mongolism in the population, that is to say about 1 in 1400. (The frequency must be halved, because discordant twins may occur in two ways, the first mongol and the second normal or vice versa.) This figure must, however, be increased considerably to allow for the lack of independence due to the facts that mongolism is more frequent among older mothers and among mothers who have already had one mongol child. Carter and Evans (1961) found 5 mongols among 312 births following the birth of a mongol child. The expected frequency of concordant dizygotic twins is probably about half this frequency, that is to say about one per cent.

The degree of concordance in the postulated third type of twins must be considered with some care. If these twins are uniovular dispermatic, derived from the division of the ovum before fertilization, they will be concordant if the chromosome abnormality is in the ovum and discordant if it is in one of the spermatozoa. The same rule applies to secondary oocytary twins if mongolism is due to translocation or to non-disjunction at the first meiotic division, but if non-disjunction occurs in the ovum at the second meiotic division, one of the products of this division will contain no 21 chromosome and will probably be inviable so that secondary oocytary twins will not develop. On the other hand, primary oocytary twins will probably be inviable for the same reason if the chromosomal abnormality is due to non-disjunction in the ovum at the first meiotic division or to translocation on the mother's side, and will be discordant otherwise. In brief, therefore, uniovular dispermatic and secondary oocytary twins should often be concordant while primary oocytary twins will not be concordant. If uniovular dispermatic or secondary oocytary twins exist there should therefore be an increase in the frequency of concordant unlike-sexed twins above the frequency of one per cent expected by chance.

A considerable amount of information about mongolism in twins has been accumulated and is summarized in Table 1.5

Table 1.5. Mongolism in twins

	Concordant	Discordant	Total
Like-sexed	38	111	149
Unlike-sexed	3	98	101

(Smith 1955, Allen and Baroff 1955, Keay 1958, Hanhart 1960, McDonald 1964). The preponderance of like-sexed twins among the concordant pairs indicates that nearly all of them are monozygotic. One of the cases of unlike-sexed concordant twins was reported by Nicholson and Keay (1957) and two by McDonald (1964), although the diagnosis is open to question in one of them (McDonald, personal communication). The frequency of concordance among unlike-sexed twins can therefore be estimated as two or three per cent, which is not appreciably greater than the frequency of one per cent predicted on the assumption that they are all dizygotic, particularly when it is remembered that most of these cases have been obtained from individual case reports in the literature in which concordant unlike-sexed twins are likely to be over-represented because of their rarity interest. Furthermore, Nicholson and Keay (1957) did a large number of blood-group determinations on their unlike-sexed concordant pair from which it can be concluded that the twins differ on the mother's side in at least one blood group system (the Duffy system) and therefore cannot be uniovular dispermatic twins. The evidence from mongolism therefore indicates that neither uniovular dispermatic nor secondary oocytary twins occur with appreciable frequency in man. (It may be noted in passing that the frequency of monozygotic twins in Table 1.5 is about 38/250 or fourteen per cent, which is only about half the expected frequency. However, if the concordant pairs are counted twice instead of once, as they should be under complete ascertainment, the frequency of monozygotic twins becomes 76/291 or twenty six per cent. A slight excess of dizygotic twins is expected because of the increased age of mothers of mongols.)

In summary, several lines of investigation have failed to reveal any evidence of the existence of a third type of twinning in man. It can be concluded that such twins must be rather rare if they occur at all and that nearly all, if not all, non-identical twins are dizygotic. It must be mentioned, however that dizygotic twins may have different fathers and may thus only be as alike as half-sibs if a woman has had intercourse with two men in a short period of time. In 1810 Archer reported that he had observed a white woman who had had intercourse with a white man and a negro within a short period and who was delivered of twins, one of which was white and the other a mulatto. More recently Andreassi (1947) has discussed the case of a married woman who had extra-marital intercourse and who was delivered of a boy-girl pair of twins; by examination of their blood groups it was shown that the husband was the father of the boy and the other man of the girl. This phenomenon of superfecundation by different men must, however, be very rare. (Superfecundation is the fertilization of two ova released simultaneously by spermatozoa released in different coital acts. Superfoetation, on the other hand, is the fertilization of two ova released in different menstrual cycles. Conclusive evidence has never been obtained of the occurrence of superfoetation which would require the suppression of the inhibition of the corpus luteum of the first pregnancy on subsequent ovulation.)

Appendix: The Diagnosis of Zygosity

It seems likely that an experienced observer can classify twins as monozygotic or dizygotic with considerable accuracy by assessing their physical similarity, but it is often desirable to use a more objective method based on the determination of blood groups together with other characters whose mode of inheritance is well established. This method was outlined by Race and Sanger (1954) and was developed further by Smith and Penrose (1955), and by Sutton, Clark, and Schull (1955); the logical basis of the method has also been discussed by Bulmer (1958).

The method employed by the above authors is as follows. We first calculate L_M and L_D, the likelihoods of obtaining the observed phenotypes of the twins given the phenotypes of all the relatives studied, on the hypotheses that the twins are monozygotic and dizygotic respectively. We then multiply these likelihoods by m and d, respectively, the known relative frequencies of monozygotic and dizygotic twins in the general population; for Caucasoid populations we may write, approximately, $m = 0.004$, $d = 0.008$, but if the age of the mother when the twins were born is known it is preferable to use the age-specific twinning rates. We then assert, using Bayes' theorem, that P_M, the posterior probability of the twins being monozygotic, is $mL_M/(mL_M+dL_D)$ and that P_D, the posterior probability of the twins being dizygotic, is $dL_D/(mL_M+dL_D)$. In order to calculate these probabilities it is only necessary to know the ratio, dL_D/mL_M, which represents the relative odds in favour of the twins being dizygotic. Since the prior probabilities are known relative frequencies, the posterior probabilities have the following frequency interpretation: in the population of all families having phenotypes identical with those of the observed family, the proportion of monozygotic twins is P_M and the proportion of dizygotic twins is P_D.

For example, let us suppose that the family consists of father, mother, a pair of girl twins, and another child, and that they have been tested for the ABO, MN, and Rhesus blood groups with the following results:

Father	A;	M;	Rh$^+$
Mother	O;	MN;	Rh$^-$
Single child	O;	MN;	Rh$^-$
Girl twins	O;	MN;	Rh$^+$

From the blood groups of the single child the father must have the genotype AO; MM; Rr. The genotypes of both parents are therefore known and we can calculate the likelihoods of getting the observed phenotypes of the twins, on the alternative hypotheses that they are monozygotic and dizygotic, as follows:

Character	L_M	L_D	L_D/L_M
Sex	$\frac{1}{2}$	$\frac{1}{4}$	$\frac{1}{2}$
ABO	$\frac{1}{2}$	$\frac{1}{4}$	$\frac{1}{2}$
MN	$\frac{1}{2}$	$\frac{1}{4}$	$\frac{1}{2}$
Rhesus	$\frac{1}{2}$	$\frac{1}{4}$	$\frac{1}{2}$
Total	$\frac{1}{16}$	1/256	$\frac{1}{16}$

If we assume that $d/m = 2$ then the odds *against* the twins being dizygotic are 8:1 so that $P_M = 8/9$ and $P_D = 1/9$. More information could of course be obtained by examining further blood groups.

In the above example the genotypes of both parents could be deduced from their phenotypes together with the phenotype of the single child. However, if the single child had been Rh$^+$ we would not have known for certain whether the father was RR or Rr and we would have had to argue as follows. The frequency of Rh$^-$ individuals in the population is about sixteen per cent, from which the frequency of the r gene can be estimated as $(0\cdot16)^{\frac{1}{2}} = 0\cdot4$. (This follows from the Hardy-Weinberg law which states that if the frequencies of the R and r genes are p and q respectively, then the frequencies of the genotypes RR, Rr, and rr in a population mating at random are p^2, $2pq$, and q^2.) The frequencies of the genotypes RR, Rr, and rr can therefore be estimated as $0\cdot36$, $0\cdot48$, and $0\cdot16$ respectively, from which it follows that among Rh$^+$ individuals about 3/7 are RR and 4/7 Rr. Furthermore the frequency of RR men among Rh$^+$ men married to Rh$^-$ women who have one Rh$^+$ child is $0\cdot6$, since such parents will always have Rh$^+$ children if the father is RR whereas their chance of having a Rh$^+$ child if the father is Rr is $\frac{1}{2}$; the result follows from Bayes' theorem. We can now calculate the likelihood that a pair of twins produced by such parents will both be Rh$^+$; this likelihood is $0\cdot6 + \frac{1}{2} \times 0\cdot4 = 0\cdot8$ if the twins are monozygotic and $0\cdot6 + \frac{1}{4} \times 0\cdot4$ if they are dizygotic. The likelihood ratio would therefore be $0\cdot7/0\cdot8 = 0\cdot875$ instead of $0\cdot5$.

A similar method can be used to calculate the likelihoods when the parental blood groups are not known. To illustrate the method we shall calculate the likelihood that both twins are of group M. Such twins can be produced by three mating types, $MM \times MM$, $MM \times MN$, and $MN \times MN$, the frequencies of which will be:

$$p^2 \times p^2 = p^4, \quad 2 \times p^2 \times 2pq = 4p^3q, \text{ and } 2pq \times 2pq = 4p^2q^2$$

where p is the frequency of the M gene; the factor 2 occurs for the mating type $MM \times MN$ since this includes the two possibilities that the father is MM and the mother MN or vice versa. The chances of obtaining an M child from these matings are 1, $\frac{1}{2}$, and $\frac{1}{4}$ respectively. The likelihood that a pair of dizygotic twins will be of group M is therefore

$$p^4 + p^3q + \tfrac{1}{4}p^2q^2 = p^2(1 - \tfrac{1}{2}q)^2$$

whereas the likelihood for monozygotic twins is p^2; the likelihood ratio is $(1 - \tfrac{1}{2}q)^2$ which is equal to $0\cdot59$ if q is given its typical European value of 0·47. Tables of the likelihood ratio for all the common blood groups have been calculated by Smith and Penrose (1955).

In addition to the blood groups and similar discrete characters valuable information can be obtained from several continuous physical characters whose mode of inheritance is well known and which are largely under genetic control. The most important of these characters is the total finger ridge count, which will be discussed further in Chapter 7. If d is the difference in ridge count between a pair of twins then the variance of d is $2\sigma^2(1-\rho)$, where σ is the standard deviation of ridge count in the population, which is about 52 (Holt 1955), and ρ is the correlation between twins, which is about 0·95 for monozygotic and 0·475 for dizygotic twins (see Chapter 7). The standard deviation of d is therefore about 16 for monozygotic and 53 for dizygotic twins. If d is approximately normally distributed, which is a reasonable assumption since its distribution will certainly be symmetrical even though the underlying distribution is slightly skew, then the likelihood of an observed value of d can be calculated as $\phi(d/16)/16$ for monozygotic twins and $\phi(d/53)/53$ for dizygotic twins, where ϕ is the standard normal density function. If $d = 10$, for example, the likelihood ratio can be calculated as 0·36. This method can obviously be extended to other continuous characters.

The method of calculating the likelihood for blood groups described in the last paragraph can also be used to find the probability of concordance for dizygotic twins. The calculation of the probability of concordance for the MN blood groups is set out in Table 1.6. The frequencies of the different possible mating types are shown in the second column, on the assumptions that mating occurs at random and that the frequencies of the three genotypes obey the Hardy-Weinberg law. Multiplying these probabilities by the conditional probability of concordance for a given mating type and adding over the possible mating types we obtain the predicted concordance of $1 - \frac{1}{2}pq(4-3pq)$, which is equal to 0·59 if we substitute the values of $p = 0·53$

and $q = 0.47$ typical of European populations. This method can obviously be extended to find the predicted concordance of the other blood-group systems shown in Table 1.2, depending on the mode of inheritance of the system and the frequencies of the alleles in the population.

We shall finally consider the distribution of the number of

Table 1.6. *Calculation of the expected concordance of dizygotic twins in the MN blood groups*

Parental genotypes	Frequency	Probability of concordant twins	Product
$MM \times MM$	p^4	1	p^4
$MM \times MN$	$4p^3q$	$\frac{1}{2}$	$2p^3q$
$MM \times NN$	$2p^2q^2$	1	$2p^2q^2$
$MN \times MN$	$4p^2q^2$	$\frac{3}{8}$	$1\frac{1}{2}p^2q^2$
$MN \times NN$	$4pq^3$	$\frac{1}{2}$	$2pq^3$
$NN \times NN$	q^4	1	q^4
Total			$1 - \frac{1}{2}pq(4 - 3pq)$

differences in four blood group systems shown in Table 1.3. The expected proportions of dizygotic twins who will be alike in the ABO, MN, Rhesus, and haptoglobin groups have been calculated by the above method and are respectively 0·62, 0·59, 0·49, and 0·61. Hence the expected proportion who will be alike in all four groups is the product of these probabilities, which is 0·109. (This probability would drop to 0·05 if the Gm serum group were included, but this cannot be done here because only those twins alike in the other groups were tested for this group.) The expected proportion who should differ in only one group is obtained by adding the probabilities of the four different ways in which this event can happen (unlike in ABO but alike in the other groups, unlike in MN but alike in the other groups, and so on). In this way we obtain the distribution shown in Table 1.7.

Table 1.7. *Distribution of the number of differences in four blood group systems among dizygotic twins*

Number of differences	0	1	2	3	4
Probability	0·109	0·327	0·360	0·173	0·031

Omitting the first group, which contains both monozygotic and dizygotic twins, and dividing by 0·891 to make the probabilities add up to 1, we obtain the predicted distribution among the remainder shown in Table 1.8. Multiplying by 108, the observed

Table 1.8. Truncated distribution omitting the group with no differences

Number of differences	0	1	2	3	4
Probability	—	0·367	0·404	0·194	0·035

number of twins with at least one difference, we obtain the expected frequencies shown in Table 1.3. The predicted distribution in Table 1.4 was obtained in the same way except that the group with no differences could be included since the twins were known to be non-identical on other grounds.

2 The Embryology of Twinning

In the last chapter it was shown that there exist two types of twins, monozygotic twins derived from the division of the embryo at some stage in its development after fertilization, and dizygotic twins derived from the independent release and subsequent fertilization of two ova. In this chapter we shall consider in more detail how and why these two types of twins arise. We shall consider first the origin of monozygotic twins, and begin by discussing the foetal membranes of twins, which provide valuable evidence about the stage of development at which monozygotic twins arise.

The foetal membranes

To understand how the foetal membranes of monozygotic twins are formed and how they cast light on the origin of the twins we must first describe briefly the development of the membranes in the normal embryo. Fig. 2.1 is a diagrammatic representation of the early stages in the development of the embryo. After fertilization the zygote divides repeatedly to form two-celled, four-celled, eight-celled, and sixteen-celled stages (Fig. 2.1, (a) and (b)); the sixteen-celled stage, which is reached by about the fourth day, is called a morula from its resemblance to a mulberry. Fluid is now secreted into the morula and forms a hollow cavity in its centre; this stage, which is reached by about the sixth day, is known as the blastocyst (Fig. 2.1 (c)). The blastocyst is formed of two parts, an outer shell of cells, the trophoblast, and the inner cell mass which is situated inside the trophoblast at one pole of the blastocyst and which is destined to become the embryo proper; the trophoblast will later form the chorion, or outer foetal membrane, and the foetal contribution to the placenta.

Until now the embryo has been surrounded by a thick membrane, the zona pellucida, which was originally formed around

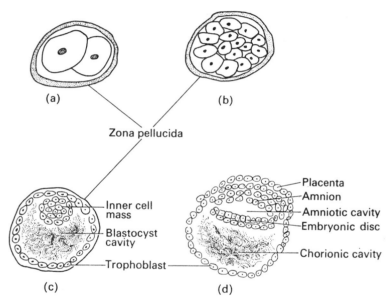

FIG. 2.1. Early stages in the development of the embryo.

(a) Two-celled stage, day 1;   (b) morula, day 4;
(c) blastocyst, day 6;   (d) early implantation, day 11.

the ovum in the ovary, and has been floating freely either in the Fallopian tube or in the uterus. On about the seventh day the zona pellucida disappears and the embryo begins to implant itself in the tissues of the uterus. Shortly after implantation has begun a cavity appears in the inner cell mass which separates the precursor of the amnion above from the embryonic disc below (Fig. 2.1 (d)); the embryo proper is derived from the embryonic disc while the amnion later becomes a smooth membrane which completely surrounds the embryo in a fluid bath.

There are thus two membranes surrounding the foetus, the chorion and the amnion. The chorion develops from the trophoblast which is differentiated towards the end of the first week of foetal life, while the amnion, which lies inside the chorion and immediately surrounds the foetus, is not differentiated until the second week. There are therefore three critical stages at which the division of the embryo to form monozygotic twins may occur. If the division occurs at the two-celled stage, by separation and independent development of the two cells, or at some stage up to the morula stage before the differentiation of the trophoblast, the twins will develop separate choria and amnia and will be embryologically indistinguishable from dizygotic twins which have developed from the fertilization of different ova. If the inner cell mass divides into two after the differentiation of the trophoblast but before that of the amnion, the resulting twins will have a common chorion but separate amnia. Finally, if the division occurs in the embryonic disc after the differentiation of the amnion the twins will have a common chorion and amnion.

The placentation of twins is illustrated diagrammatically in Fig. 2.2. The placentae of dichorial twins will be separate, as in Fig. 2.2 (a), if the embryos become implanted far apart in the uterus, but they may become fused, as in Fig. 2.2 (b), if the embryos are implanted close together; in the latter case the membranes dividing the twins will be composed of amnion-chorion-chorion-amnion. Dichorial twins may be either dizygotic twins or monozygotic twins which divided in the first few days of pregnancy. If the division occurs towards the end of the first or the beginning of the second week of pregnancy the twins will be monochorial, diamniotic as in Fig. 2.2 (c); in this case the placenta must be single and the membrane dividing the twins will be formed of two layers of amnion only. Finally, if the division occurs after the middle of the second week of

pregnancy the placenta will be of the monochorial, monoamniotic type (Fig. 2.2 (d)) in which no membrane divides the
twins.

) The chief difficulty in determining the type of placentation
in practice lies in distinguishing between a fused dichorial

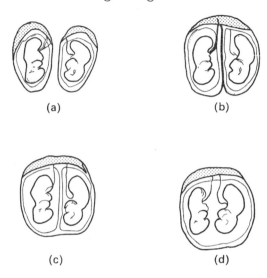

(a)   (b)

(c)   (d)

FIG. 2.2. Placentation of twins.

(a) Two choria, two amnia, separate placentae; (b) two choria, two
amnia, fused placenta; (c) one chorion, two amnia; (d) one chorion,
one amnion.

placenta (Fig. 2.2 (b)) and a monochorial, diamniotic placenta
(Fig. 2.2 (c)). Strong and Corney (1967) summarize the difference
between these two types of placenta as follows: 'The components
[of the dividing membranes] are usually apparent from a
naked-eye examination. In a monochorial placenta, the two
layers of amnion appear translucent and peel away from each
other as far as the umbilical cord, leaving no membrane in
between. In a dichorial placenta, the septum is more opaque,
and stripping the amnia leaves either a single fused or two
separate layers of chorion firmly attached to the foetal surface
of the placenta. Histology of the dividing membranes is more

time-consuming but gives an almost infallible result.' The histology of the foetal membranes is considered in detail by Bourne (1962).

Another difficulty of interpretation arises from the fact that in some mammals the chorial membranes between a pair of twins may fuse together and then disappear entirely, converting a dichorial into an apparently monochorial placenta. The best-known example is provided by cattle in which Lillie (1917) showed that nearly all twins have a monochorial, diamniotic placenta despite the fact that most of them are dizygotic. The single chorion is formed by the fusion and disappearance of the chorial dividing membranes early in foetal life and leads to the formation of vascular anastomoses between the twins; if they are of opposite sex the female twin becomes a sterile free-martin because the sex hormones from the male twin inhibit the differentiation of its sexual organs. Lillie also showed that sheep twins are usually monochorial for the same reason but that the blood vessels do not anastomose and so the female is normal in unlike-sexed pairs; it has since been shown that free-martins sometimes occur in sheep (Stormont, Weir, and Lane 1953). Rather more surprising is the situation in the marmoset in which nearly every pregnancy results in the birth of dizygotic, monochorial twins (Wislocki 1939). The single chorion results, as in the case of dizygotic cattle and sheep twins, from the fusion and disappearance of the chorial dividing membranes early in foetal life, and there is also considerable anastomosis of the foetal circulations, but there is no free-martin effect in female marmosets from unlike-sexed pairs; it seems that the foetal male sex hormone is less powerful in primates than in ungulates, as is confirmed by the fact that unlike-sexed human chimaerae twins are sexually normal and completely fertile.

This disappearance of the chorial dividing membranes in these mammals which usually bear either twins or singletons might lead us to expect the same in man, but in fact it seems rather rare, at least among dizygotic twins, and hence presumably among dichorial monozygotic twins. In a total of 763 pairs of dizygotic twins reported in six investigations (Steiner 1935, Vermelin and Ribon 1949, Potter and Fuller 1949, Potter 1963, Edwards and Cameron 1967, Strong and Corney 1967) there were only two apparently monochorial pairs (Potter and Fuller 1949), and even they might have been dichorial since the placentae were not examined histologically. It can be concluded that disappearance of the chorial dividing membranes and the consequent conversion of a dichorial into a monochorial placenta occurs rarely if at all in man. Towards the end of pregnancy, however, the adjacent chorial membranes in a dichorial placenta may fuse together to form a single layer and may then thin out so much as to give the impression to the naked eye that only amniotic tissue is present in the dividing membrane. For this reason microscopic examination of the membranous wall is necessary before the absence of chorial tissue may be accepted as certain (Corner 1955, Bourne 1962).

It is also possible that monoamniotic twins might arise by fusion and subsequent disappearance of the amniotic dividing membranes in a diamniotic, monochorial placenta. This is a difficult question to answer because monoamniotic twins are rather rare and are always monozygotic, but most obstetricians believe that monoamniotic twins do not arise in this way but by division of the embryo after the formation of the amnion. This belief is supported by the facts that the cords of such twins arise very close together (Corner 1955) and that the amniotic dividing membranes are always separate and show no signs of fusion in diamniotic, monochorial placentae. Furthermore, even in species such as cattle, sheep, and marmosets, in which the chorial dividing membranes disappear, this is not followed by disappearance of the amniotic dividing membranes, and each foetus is enclosed in its own amnion.

It can be concluded that the type of placenta in monozygotic twins probably provides a reliable guide to the stage of development at which the division of the embryo occurred. We shall consider first the frequency of monochorial and dichorial placentae in monozygotic twins; it will be remembered that monozygotic twins will be dichorial if they arise from a division which occurred before the differentiation of the trophoblast (from which the chorion is derived) towards the end of the first week of pregnancy and monochorial if they arise from a division which occurred after that time.

The results of ten investigations on the chorial types of monozygotic twins are summarized in Table 2.1. There is some

Table 2.1. *The frequency of dichorial and monochorial placentae in monozygotic twins*

Di-chorial	Mono-chorial	Per cent dichorial	Method of zygosity diagnosis	Reference
24	32	43	Physical similarity	Steiner 1935
21	52	28	,, ,,	Voûte 1935
18	43	30	,, ,,	Essen-Möller 1941
13	52	20	Blood groups	Corney, Robson and Strong 1968
44	116	28	Blood groups and Weinberg's method	Edwards and Cameron 1967
33	119	22	Weinberg's method	Essen-Möller 1941
69	109	30	,, ,,	Vermelin and Ribon 1949
22	46	32	,, ,,	Potter and Fuller 1949
33	77	30	,, ,,	Benirschke 1961
77	117	40	,, ,,	Potter 1963
354	763	32		Total

variability in the proportion of dichorial twins because of the small size of the samples, but it is no greater than would be expected from random sampling errors. In the first five investigations in the table the twins were diagnosed as monozygotic either by physical similarity in childhood or by blood-group determinations. There may be a slight bias in favour of dichorial twins in these data because they do not include twins who were stillborn or who died in infancy; as we shall see in the next chapter the death rate is higher in monochorial than in dichorial twins in this period so that the proportion of dichorial twins may be slightly lower at birth than among twins who survive into childhood. The last five investigations in Table 2.1 include data on all twins, whether live or stillborn, but only their sex type is known; the number of dichorial monozygotic twins has been estimated as the difference between the numbers of like-sexed and unlike-sexed dichorial twins, while all the monochorial twins have been assumed to be monozygotic since, with two exceptions in the data of Potter and Fuller (1949), they were all like-sexed. There is no appreciable difference between the two types of investigation, and it can be concluded that about one-third of all monozygotic twins are dichorial.

We turn now to the number of amnia. Twin pregnancies with a single amnion are rather rare. The results of ten investigations are summarized in Table 2.2 and show that the frequency of

Table 2.2. The frequency of monoamniotic twins

Monoamniotic twins	All twins	Reference
3	236	Steiner 1935
0	210	Potter and Fuller 1949
4	100	Wenner 1956
3	130	Librach and Terrin 1957
3	246	Kirk and Callagan 1960
5	824	Raphael 1961
3	250	Benirschke 1961
1	567	Potter 1963
3	326	Corney, Robson and Strong 1968
18	581	Wharton, Edwards and Cameron 1968
43	3470	Total

monoamniotic twins among all twins is just over one per cent. Since monoamniotic twins are all monozygotic and since about one third of all twins are monozygotic, it can be concluded that the frequency of monoamniotic twins among monozygotic twins is about four per cent.

Monoamniotic twins arise from division of the embryo after the formation of the amnion towards the end of the second week of pregnancy. They are usually separate, but incomplete division of the embryo at this stage sometimes gives rise to conjoined (Siamese) twins. Conjoined twins are rare, but it is difficult to obtain a precise estimate of their frequency. Potter (1960) reports that two sets of conjoined twins were delivered at the Chicago Lying-in Hospital between 1931 and 1961 in the course of over 100 000 deliveries; another set was found among the abortions. It must be borne in mind, however, that hospital statistics tend to exaggerate the incidence of twinning because of preferential admission. The Registrar-General's Statistical Review of England and Wales records that 50 sets of conjoined twins were stillborn in a total of 5 116 000 births in the years 1961–6, but to these must be added an unknown number which were born alive even though they only lived a few hours. It seems reasonable to conclude that the frequency of conjoined twins is rather more than 1 in every 100 000 births; this is equivalent to about 1 in every 400 monozygotic twin maternities.

It can be concluded that about one third of all monozygotic twins are dichorial; these twins presumably divided at or before the morula stage, that is to say before about the fifth day of foetal life. Of the remaining two thirds which are mono-chorial nearly all are diamniotic; they must have divided after the morula stage but before the differentiation of the amnion, that is to say between about the fifth and the tenth days of foetal life. Only a very small proportion of monozygotic twins, of the order of four per cent, are monoamniotic; it is likely that these twins divided soon after the differentiation of the amnion and of the embryonic disc, perhaps between the tenth and the fourteenth days of pregnancy. Most of these mono-amniotic twins are separate but some of them, perhaps about five per cent, fail to divide completely and are conjoined.

It is also of interest to consider the number of placentae. Monochorial twins must have a single placenta, but dichorial twins can either have two placentae or a single placenta formed by the fusion of two placentae (Fig. 2.2); whether or not the placentae fuse depends on whether the embryos become implanted close together or far apart in the uterus. Table 2.3

Table 2.3. *The frequency of a single, fused placenta in dichorial twins*
(Steiner 1935, Strong and Corney 1967)

Type of twin	Fused placenta	Separate placentae	Per cent with fused placenta
Mono-zygotic	21	28	43
Dizygotic	124	169	42

summarizes the results of two investigations on the frequency
of a single, fused placenta in dichorial twins. It will be seen that
the frequency is no higher among monozygotic than among
dizygotic twins, provided of course that they are dichorial. This
fact confirms that monozygotic dichorial twins are formed by
division of the embryo before implantation; it also indicates
that the zona pellucida which surrounds the embryo for the
first few days of its existence must have disappeared sufficiently
long before implantation to allow the twins to become implanted
in independent positions in the uterus.

The most important consequence of the method of placentation is its effect on the foetal circulation. In about ninety per
cent of monochorial placentae there is some sort of connection
between the foetal circulations of the twins (Strong and Corney
1967). The two commonest types of connection are: (1) a
connection between the umbilical arteries of the twins running
between the two cords on the surface of the placenta, and (2)
an arterio-venous shunt between the foetal circulations whereby an artery from one foetus supplies a cotyledon of the
placenta which is drained by a vein from the other foetus. Such
an arterio-venous shunt, if it is not compensated by a flow of
blood the other way, means that one twin is bleeding slowly
into the other twin and causes the 'transfusion syndrome'
in which the transfused twin is plethoric while the transfusing
twin is pale and anaemic because of the difference in haemoglobin values between them. The heart and kidneys are usually
much larger in the plethoric twin, who may also have hydramnios; there is often, but not invariably, a considerable

difference in birth weight between the twins. It has been estimated that between fifteen and thirty per cent of monochorial twins suffer from the transfusion syndrome to a greater or lesser degree (Rausen, Seki, and Strauss 1965, Strong and Corney 1967, Benirschke and Driscoll 1967). Even apart from this factor it is likely that an interconnected foetal circulation will be an inefficient vascular arrangement in monochorial twins. In dichorial twins, on the other hand, the foetal circulations are almost never connected; it has been estimated that the frequency of vascular communications in fused dichorial placentae is between 1 in 100 and 1 in 1 000 (Strong and Corney 1967). When such a connection occurs in dizygotic twins it probably gives rise to the blood chimaerism mentioned in the previous chapter. In monoamniotic twins the cords frequently become twisted together or knotted; this usually leads to their death and accounts for the very high mortality in such twins.

The causes of monozygotic twinning

We must now consider why the embryo sometimes divides into two at this early stage in its life history. This is a difficult question to answer since the frequency of monozygotic twinning is remarkably constant under a wide range of conditions; as we shall see in Chapter 4, the only factor which seems to influence it at all is the age of the mother. However, it is likely that the constancy of the monozygotic twinning rate in man is due to the constancy of the environment in which the mammalian embryo develops and to its protection from outside disturbance. In non-mammalian eggs such as fish eggs which develop outside the mother the frequency of monozygotic twinning is much more labile and can be altered more easily by changes in the external environment. Furthermore, it is very difficult to detect the occurrence of monozygotic twins in multiparous mammals like rats and guinea pigs on which experiments are usually done. We must therefore rely largely on experiments in non-viviparous species to study the factors which lead to monozygotic twinning.

In 1921, Stockard, who had worked mainly on fish eggs, put

forward the theory that all types of congenital abnormalities which are not hereditary are due to developmental arrest and that the type of abnormality which resulted from such arrest depended not on the agent which caused it but on the developmental stage at which the arrest occurred; the tissues or organs which were proliferating most actively at that time would be most likely to develop abnormally when growth resumed. On this interpretation monozygotic twinning is to be regarded as a congenital abnormality caused by developmental arrest occurring very early in embryonic life before tissue differentiation has begun. Stockard based this theory on the fact that he could produce twinning experimentally in the eggs of the sea minnow and of trout by retarding their development at a very early stage, by depriving them of oxygen or keeping them at a low temperature; the same treatments at a later stage in development produced localized congenital abnormalities such as cyclopia (the presence of a single, central eye). Similar results have been obtained in starfish (Newman 1923) and in chickens (Sturkie 1946).

As evidence that this theory applied to mammals, Stockard considered the method of reproduction in the armadillo. As we saw in the last chapter, the nine-banded armadillo regularly produces monozygotic quadruplets, and the mulita armadillo normally produces eight or more offspring derived from a single ovum. It is therefore of interest that implantation of the ovum is delayed in both these species. The nine-banded armadillo mates in July and the ovum develops to the blastocyst stage in about a week. It does not, however, become implanted immediately but remains quiescent until early November, when it implants, divides into four and then develops normally until birth in March or April (Newman 1917, Hamlett 1932). There is probably a similar quiescent period in the mulita armadillo, although the evidence is indirect (Hamlett 1932).

Stockard's interpretation of these facts is that the division of the embryo into four embryos in one species and into eight or more in the other is a direct consequence of the developmental arrest during the long period of quiescence, which is in turn due to lack of oxygen caused by the failure of the embryo to become implanted immediately. This interpretation was attacked by Hamlett in 1933, mainly on the grounds that delayed implantation is also known to occur in roe deer and in badgers, but is not accompanied by monozygotic twinning in either case. This criticism had in fact been foreseen by Stockard, who suggested that either the period of quiescence in the deer occurred at a time when the embryo was insensitive to it, or that the deer embryo only possessed a slight genetic tendency to divide compared with the armadillo. Further light is thrown on this argument by a discussion of the evolutionary reasons for the development of delayed implantation.

It is likely that in most species in which it occurs delayed implantation has arisen as an evolutionary adaptation to lengthen the period of gestation in order that both mating and birth may occur at favourable periods of the year. Many species of seal come ashore once a year during the summer to breed, when the females give birth to their young, suckle them, and then mate over a period of six to eight weeks (Harrison 1963). If implantation were not delayed it would be necessary for the seals to come ashore a second time during the winter in order to mate, which would obviously be disadvantageous. In terrestrial mammals in which implantation is delayed, such as the badger and the roe deer, mating occurs during the spring or summer and is followed by a quiescent period until the winter when the embryo implants, develops, and is born in the early spring. It has been plausibly suggested that in these species delayed implantation is an adaptation which allows birth in the early spring when the young have the longest time to develop to maturity before the onset of winter, without requiring mating to occur in the winter, which might be unsuitable as a breeding season because of climatic conditions and a shortage of food (Fries 1880). However, as Hamlett (1935) pointed out, this explanation presupposes severe winter conditions which are unfavourable both to survival of the young and to mating, and cannot be applied to tropical species such as the armadillo.

A clue to the simultaneous development of polyembryony (division of the embryo) and delayed implantation in some armadillos may possibly be provided by their evolutionary history. Armadillos, together with ant-eaters and sloths, belong to a rather aberrant order of mammals called the Edentates which live in South America. It seems likely that the production of a single offspring is the primitive condition in this order; all members of the order have a single, undivided uterus, which is usually regarded as an adaptation to producing single young, and single births are the rule in ant-eaters and sloths (Asdell 1964). Several species of armadillo, however, produce more than one young at a time. In the genus *Dasypus*, represented by the nine-banded armadillo (*D. novemcinctus*) and the mulita armadillo (*D. hybridus*), polyembryony is the rule, as we have already seen. In the genus *Euphractus*, on the other hand, dizygotic twins are usual. In *E. villosus*, Fernandez (1915) observed twenty-nine twins and five singletons in thirty-four pregnant females, and inferred that the twins were dizygotic from the fact that in ten pairs which he was able to sex, seven pairs were of unlike sex and only three pairs were like-sexed. In *E. sexcinctus*, the reports summarized by Asdell (1964) together with reports by Chapman (1901) and Newman (1917) give a total of three single births, six twins, and one triplet; it seems likely, although there is no direct evidence, that the twins are dizygotic as in *E. villosus*. Data on other species are rather scanty, but it is probable that single births are the rule in the giant armadillo, *Priodontes giganteus*, and in the genus *Tolypeutes* (Asdell 1964; Newman 1917).

It seems reasonable to suggest that it was originally advantageous for the Edentates to produce single offspring, possibly because they were tree-dwellers as Romer (1959) suggests, but that the way of life adopted by the armadillos, in particular their habit of constructing burrows in which the young can be nursed, has made it advantageous for them to produce larger litters. (The evolutionary significance of litter size will be discussed more fully in Chapter 8.) This challenge has been met in the genus *Euphractus* by increasing the number of ova released from the ovary, and in the genus *Dasypus* by polyembryony. It may also be suggested that, if delayed implantation favours subsequent division of the ovum, then it may have evolved as a side-product of selection for polyembryony in the genus *Dasypus*. The absence of polyembryony in other species in which delayed implantation occurs may be due to selection against it since the optimal litter size has already been reached. However, this argument is highly speculative, and it is quite possible that the association of polyembryony and delayed implantation in the armadillo is just a coincidence.

It has been claimed that there is direct evidence for Stockard's theory in man. The ovum sometimes becomes implanted in the Fallopian tube before it reaches the uterus, and Arey (1922) has shown that in a series of unilateral tubal twin pregnancies the proportion of monochorial to dichorial twins is about fifteen times as great as it is in uterine pregnancies; he concluded that monozygotic twinning is more likely to occur in tubal than in uterine pregnancy, and he explained this by supposing that the unfavourable conditions in tubal pregnancy lead to twinning. There is, however, a serious flaw in this argument. By excluding bilateral tubal twin pregnancies Arey must have excluded many dizygotic but no monozygotic twins; and by excluding pregnanacies in which one twin occurred in the tube and the other in the uterus he must have excluded many dichorial but no monochorial twins. Both these sources of bias would lead one to expect a high proportion of monochorial twins in unilateral tubal twin pregnancies.

Another finding which is of interest in this context is that the frequency of congenital malformations is about twice as high in monozygotic twins as in single births, while there is no increase in dizygotic twins (Heady and Heasman 1955, Barr and Stevenson 1961, Stevenson, Johnston, Stewart, and Golding 1966). It is tempting to attribute this fact to a common factor

4

which is responsible both for monozygotic twinning and congenital malformations, but it might equally well be due to less favourable conditions in monochorial placentae.

In conclusion, there is strong experimental evidence that developmental retardation at a very early stage caused by factors such as lack of oxygen can lead to monozygotic twinning in lower vertebrates; and it seems reasonable to regard this type of twinning as similar in its aetiology to the congenital abnormalities. But these considerations do not take us very far towards explaining why a particular embryo should divide in this way. It is true that this division occurs at a stage in development just before or during implantation, when the embryo may be running short of oxygen or nutrients; but there is no direct evidence that this is the cause of monzygotic twinning in mammals, although some circumstantial evidence is provided by the simultaneous occurrence of polyembryony and delayed implantation in two species of armadillo.

The causes of dizygotic twinning

Dizygotic twins result from the release from the ovaries of two ova which are both fertilized and which both develop to birth. A change in the dizygotic twinning rate can therefore be caused by a change either in the frequency of double ovulation, or in the proportion of times on which both ova are fertilized, or in foetal mortality. The rather scanty evidence available about the second and third factors will be discussed later; in this section we shall consider only the primary cause of dizygotic twinning, that is to say double ovulation.

The number of ovarian follicles which ripens during each oestrous or menstrual cycle is not an intrinsic property of the ovary but is regulated by the gonadotrophic hormone of the anterior pituitary gland. The first evidence that the ovary is controlled by some factor outside itself was obtained by John Hunter in 1787 when he took two similar sows, removed one ovary from one of them, and then allowed them to mate with the same boar. The average litter size of the half-spayed sow was almost the same as that of the normal sow, so that its single ovary must have produced nearly twice as many ova per litter as one of the ovaries of the normal sow. Hunter's experiment has been repeated in several other species with the same result. It has also been shown that the ovary of an immature animal will function normally when transplanted into a mature animal, from which it can be inferred that there is some substance present in the mature but not in the immature animal which stimulates the ovary to function.

These facts suggested that ovarian function is controlled by some factor circulating in the blood. It was first shown by Smith (1926) that this factor is a hormone secreted by the anterior pituitary gland. Removal of this gland (hypophysectomy) leads, among other things, to a cessation of ovarian function which can be reversed by implanting fresh gland or by injecting purified extracts of the gland. Such treatment also leads to sexual maturity in immature animals. The hormone responsible for this action is called gonadotrophin. (In fact there seem to be at least two gonadotrophic hormones, the follicle-stimulating hormone and the luteinizing hormone, but this complication will be ignored here; the reader is referred to standard textbooks of physiology for fuller information.)

In normal, adult animals injection of gonadotrophin leads to the release of a larger number of ova than usual; such super-ovulation has been demonstrated in many species including rabbits, rats, sheep, and cattle, and work is in progress to use this as a method of increasing productivity in farming (Hammond 1961). It has recently been shown that the same is true in man. Gemzell and Roos (1966) treated about a hundred women who had long-lasting amenorrhaea (absence of menstruation) with injections of gonadotrophin. Forty-three pregnancies resulted, of which twenty were of single children, fourteen twins, two triplets, three quadruplets, one quintuplet, two sextuplets, and one septuplet, although many of the higher multiple births were aborted; this is clearly far in excess of the usual frequency of multiple births, and there is no doubt from collateral evidence that it is due to multiple ovulation rather than polyembryony. Similar results have been obtained by other authors.

Further evidence that the frequency of double ovulation in man is controlled by the level of pituitary gonadotrophin is provided by the fact that the frequency of dizygotic twinning and the amount of gonadotrophin in the blood both increase with maternal age. This subject will be discussed more fully in Chapter 4.

Ovarian function is thus controlled by the gonadotrophic hormones of the anterior pituitary gland. Pituitary activity in its turn is controlled by the hormones oestrogen and progesterone secreted by the ovary; these ovarian hormones in fact inhibit the secretion of gonadotrophin. This is the cause of the compensatory hypertrophy of the remaining ovary after unilateral ovariectomy; when one ovary is removed the amount of ovarian hormone secreted is halved, which causes more gonadotrophin to be secreted with a resulting increase in the activity of the remaining ovary. Such a negative feed-back is typical of the self-regulating devices of the body. This inhibition of the pituitary by ovarian hormones is the principle underlying the use of oral contraceptives. For further information on this highly complicated subject the reader is again referred to standard textbooks on physiology.

The number of ova released is thus controlled by the amount of pituitary gonadotrophin, but the mechanism through which this control is exercised is far from clear. At the beginning of each menstrual cycle a number of ovarian follicles begin to develop in each ovary, but normally only one of them grows into a mature Graafian follicle destined to ovulate, while the rest at one stage or another stop growing and undergo atresia. The situation is similar in all mammals in that the number of mature Graafian follicles at the time of ovulation is much smaller than the number of ovarian follicles which begin to ripen at the beginning of the ovarian cycle. It seems likely that the atretic follicles are in some way inhibited from developing, possibly by oestrogen secreted by the developing follicles, but it is uncertain how this mechanism works or how it ensures the development of the number of mature ova characteristic of the species. However, a considerable amount of information exists about the distribution of the number of ova between the two ovaries, which may cast light on whether or not the two ovaries behave independently.

In multiparous species it has been found that the number of corpora lutea is randomly distributed between the right and the left ovaries; this has been demonstrated in the mouse, the common shrew, the lesser shrew, the bank vole, and the rabbit (Brambell 1956). It indicates that the ovaries are acting independently of each other and that the number of ova in one ovary does not affect in any way the number in the other. The mechanism which controls the number of ova which develop must be a local mechanism acting locally in each ovary (given of course a constant level of gonadotrophin). The total number of ova is the sum of two independent contributions, one from each ovary.

This principle of the independence of the two ovaries is found even in species such as the marmoset, which regularly produces twins derived from the release of one ovum from each ovary, but it clearly cannot hold in a uniparous species; to ensure that one ovum is released the two ovaries must act as a unit. Several ways of achieving this end have been adopted by uniparous species. In some bats only one ovary is functional, the left ovary in the Indian vampire bat and the right ovary in the horseshoe bats (Asdell 1964). This mechanism is not found in other orders, although one ovary may be slightly more active than the other. It is not known whether the two ovaries ovulate equally often in women, but in the Rhesus monkey Hartman (1932) found thirty-two ovulations in the left ovary compared with thirty-four in the right.

Another mechanism for converting the two ovaries into a single unit has been adopted by seals in which there is strict alternation of ovulation from one cycle to the next (Harrison,

Matthews and Roberts 1952). It seems that the corpus luteum, which persists for a considerable time, inhibits the development of Graafian follicles in its own ovary but not in the other ovary during the next cycle; there is thus only one ovary functional in each cycle. This strict alternation is not found except in seals, although there may be some tendency towards alternation. Thus Hammond (1927) found alternation in sixty-five per cent of cases in cattle, and Hartman (1932) found alternation in seventy-one per cent of cases in the Rhesus monkey, compared with a chance expectation of fifty per cent.

Uniparous species which have not suppressed the function of one ovary either permanently as in some bats or temporarily as in seals must have established some central control (presumably hormonal) whereby the development of a Graafian follicle in one ovary inhibits the development of a similar follicle in the other ovary; as we have seen, such central control does not exist in multiparous species, although they have local control whereby the Graafian follicles inhibit the development of more follicles in the same ovary. We can obtain some information about the relative importance of local and central control in uniparous species by considering the frequency with which twins, when they do occur, are derived from ova in the same ovary or in different ovaries; if central control is predominant, then twins will be equally likely to be of unilateral or of bilateral origin, while the retention of some local control will be reflected in a preponderance of bilateral twins.

In a survey of a large number of pregnant sheep uteri from packing houses, Henning (1939) found 137 cases of double corpora lutea of which 75 were unilateral and 62 bilateral, which is in reasonable agreement with the expectation of equality if central control is predominant; in a rather smaller series Marshall (1903) found 5 unilateral and 7 bilateral cases of double ovulation in sheep. In cattle the evidence is conflicting. Küpfer (1920) found 9 unilateral and 8 bilateral double ovulations, but Lillie (1917) found 22 cases of bilateral double ovulations and no unilateral cases. Further information is required, but it is possible that there are breed differences in the relative importance of central and local control. Little information is available about the relative frequency of bilateral and unilateral double ovulations in women, although it should not be too difficult to obtain; the only case known to me in which this information is available was reported by Allen, Pratt, Newell, and Bland (1930) who found two early ova after washing out the Fallopian tubes, one ovum in each tube, and verified that there was also one corpus luteum in each ovary.

In conclusion, it may be suggested that the number of mature ova released is determined by a balance between the action of pituitary gonadotrophin which stimulates the ovarian follicles to develop, and the inhibitory action exerted by ripening follicles on the development of other follicles. In multiparous species this inhibitory action is only exerted locally in the same ovary, but in uniparous species it is also extended to the other ovary, except in those species which have suppressed the function of one ovary either permanently or temporarily. In women, one Graafian follicle usually becomes dominant and inhibits all the others, but if this inhibition fails, either through excessive pituitary stimulation or for some other reason, two or more ova will be released from which dizygotic twins or higher multiple births may develop.

3 The Course and Outcome of Pregnancy

IN this chapter we shall compare the course and outcome of pregnancy in single and multiple births. It will be found that multiple pregnancies form a natural experiment that casts valuable light on the physiology of normal human pregnancy and on the causes of stillbirth and infant mortality. We shall begin by discussing the closely related subjects of birth weight and length of gestation which respectively throw light on the factors controlling foetal growth and the onset of labour. We shall then consider the reasons for the increased mortality in multiple births, and finally discuss whether there are any lasting effects on surviving twins.

Birth weight and length of gestation

It is well known that twins weigh less at birth and are born earlier than single births, and that these differences become progressively greater in triplets and quadruplets. Representative data on the birth weight and length of gestation in single and multiple births are shown in Tables 3.1 and 3.2. There is some variability, particularly in the birth weights, but in round figures it can be concluded that the mean birth weights of singletons, twins, triplets, and quadruplets are about seven, five, four, and three pounds respectively, and that the corresponding lengths of gestation are about forty, thirty-seven, thirty-five, and thirty-four weeks.

The decrease in the birth weight in multiple births is clearly due, at least in past, to the lower length of gestation. To determine the importance of this factor I have computed the standardized mean birth weight of single births with the same

Table 3.1. Mean birth weight (pounds) in multiple births

Place	Type of sample	Single	Twin	Triplet	Quad-ruplet	Reference
U.S.A. (White)	All live births	7·4	5·3	3·9		National figures, 1960
U.S.A. (Coloured)	All live births	6·9	5·0	3·8		National figures, 1960
Italy	All births	7·7	5·5			National figures, 1961
Birmingham, England	All births	7·4	5·3	4·0	3·1	McKeown and Record 1952
London, England	Hospital records	7·2	5·0			Karn 1952, Karn and Penrose 1951
Pavia, Italy	Maternity clinic	7·1	5·2			Fraccaro 1956, 1957
Singapore (Chinese)	Hospital records	6·6	5·0			Millis 1959a
Singapore (Indian)	Hospital records	6·2	4·2			Millis 1959a
Ibadan, Nigeria	Hospital records, booked cases	6·3	4·4			Lawson and Lister 1955

distribution of length of gestation as multiple births. The results of this calculation are set out in Table 3.3. It has necessarily been assumed in the standardization that the mean birth weight of babies born after a given length of gestation is

Table 3.2. Mean length of gestation (days) in multiple births

Place	Type of sample	Single	Twin	Triplet	Quad-ruplet	Reference
Birmingham, England	All births	280	262	247	237	McKeown and Record 1952
Pavia, Italy	Maternity clinic	277	255			Fraccaro 1956, 1957
London, England	Hospital records	280	257			Karn 1952, Karn and Penrose 1957
Chicago, U.S.A.	Hospital records	282	256			Potter and Crunden 1941

the same as the mean weight of all foetuses of that age. This assumption is unlikely to be true exactly because the onset of labour may be late if the foetus is small, or may be early due to adverse conditions which have also retarded the growth of the foetus; the curve of birth weight against length of gestation cannot for these reasons be used as a foetal growth curve.

Nevertheless, the magnitude of the difference between the observed weight of multiple births and the standardized weight of single births with the same distribution of length of gestation leaves no doubt that a large part of the reduction in the birth

Table 3.3. Mean birth weight (pounds) in multiple births standardized for length of gestation

Type of birth	Birth weight	Standardized birth weight (singletons)	Crude birth weight (singletons)	Reference
Twins	5·3	6·6	7·4	McKeown and Record 1952
Twins	5·0	6·6	7·2	Karn 1952
Twins	5·2	6·3	7·1	Fraccaro 1956, 1957
Triplets	4·0	5·7	7·4	McKeown and Record 1952
Quadrup.	3·1	5·0	7·4	McKeown and Record 1952

weight in multiple births is due to some factor other than the shorter length of gestation.

This conclusion is confirmed by Fig. 3.1, which shows the relationship between the birth weight and the length of gestation in two investigations. It has already been remarked that these curves cannot be regarded as foetal growth curves and that in consequence no conclusions can be drawn from their detailed shape; in any case the relationship between the curves for single and twin births is rather different in the two investigations. Nevertheless, the facts that the birth weight is lower in twins than in single births at *all* lengths of gestation, and that the same is true in higher multiple births in Fig. 3.1 (a), clearly indicate that much of the reduction in birth weight is due to some factor other than the lower length of gestation.

Before discussing what this factor may be it is interesting to consider whether there is any difference in birth weight between monochorial and dichorial twins. Several investigations have shown that the mean birth weight is slightly lower in like-sexed

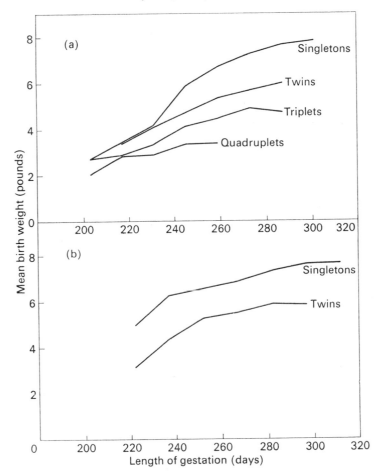

FIG. 3.1. Mean birth weight in multiple births by length of gestation (a) from McKeown and Record (1952), (b) from Karn (1952) and Karn and Penrose (1951).

than in unlike-sexed twins; the weighted average of the differences found in six studies is $0\cdot15\pm0\cdot03$ pound (Karn 1952, 1953, 1954, McKeown and Record 1952, Fraccaro 1956, Guttmacher and Kohl 1958). The most plausible explanation of this difference is that it is due to a difference between mono-chorial and dichorial twins; there is no reason why dichorial monozygotic twins should differ in their birth weight from dizygotic twins since they are embryologically indistinguishable. If this argument is accepted it is necessary to postulate a difference of about 0·45 pound between monochorial and dichorial twins, since about one-third of like-sexed twins are monochorial among Europeans. The existence of such a difference has been confirmed directly in four investigations which all show that monochorial twins are, on average, about half a pound lighter than dichorial twins (Cho 1934, de Siebenthal 1945, Potter 1963, Naeye, Benirschke, Hagstrom, and Marcus 1966); the weighted average of the differences is in fact 0·47±0·04 pound. It also seems likely, from observations on the birth weight of triplets by sex type, that similar conclusions hold good for higher multiple births (McKeown and Record 1952).

There are two possible explanations of the reduction in the birth weight of monochorial compared with dichorial twins. The first is that the placenta of such twins, being derived from only one chorion, is smaller than the combined placentae of dichorial twins which are formed from two choria. However, the rather scanty evidence available indicates that there is little difference in the combined placental weights of mono-chorial and dichorial twins (Vaccari 1908, Naeye 1964). This rather remarkable fact demonstrates clearly that foetal demand plays the dominant part in determining placental size. It there-fore seems likely that the reduction in weight in monochorial twins is a consequence not of the *size* of the placenta but of the unusual *method* of placentation, and in particular of the vascular communication between the twins discussed in the last chapter. Even apart from the transfusion syndrome it is likely that an interconnected foetal circulation will be an inefficient vascular arrangement and may well be the cause of the decreased weight of monochorial twins.

We must now consider why dichorial twins are under-weight compared with single births, even after allowance has been made for their lower length of gestation. Three explanations have been put forward to account for the retardation in foetal growth in twins and higher multiple births (Dawes 1968): (1) that overcrowding in the uterus limits the area available for placental growth and so limits the size of the foetus through placental insufficiency; (2) that the mother is unable to provide sufficient nourishment, or perhaps hormones, to support the growth of two or more foetuses at the same rate as a single foetus; (3) that the blood supply to the uterus is insufficient to support as rapid growth in multiple as in single pregnancy. On the first hypothesis reduction in placental weight, regarded as a crude index of placental sufficiency, is regarded as the cause of the reduction in foetal weight, whereas on the second and third hypotheses it would be regarded as a consequence of the reduction in foetal weight which reduces the demand on the placenta.

McKeown and Record (1953) have shown that the placental weight of twins is lower than that of singletons at all lengths of gestation, but that when foetal weight is plotted against placental weight twins are lighter than singletons with the same placental weight, even after allowing for their different lengths of gestation; in other words, the percentage reduction in placental weight in twins is smaller than the percentage reduction in foetal weight, so that the ratio of placental weight to foetal weight is higher in twins than in single births. It will be seen from Table 3.3 that the mean weight of twins is about 5·2 pounds, compared with a weight of 6·5 pounds in singletons after removing the effect of the difference in length of gestation; this represents a reduction of about twenty per cent. The corresponding figures for the placental weights of twins and singletons, calculated from the data of McKeown and Record (1953), are 1·14 and 1·30 pounds respectively, representing a reduction of twelve per cent.

McKeown and Record (1953) concluded from the above facts that the reduction in foetal weight is partly, but not entirely, accounted for by the reduction in placental weight. However, we have already seen that placental size is determined by foetal demand and we should therefore expect a reduction in placental weight if foetal growth is retarded through some other cause; the fact that the reduction in placental weight is proportionately smaller than the reduction in foetal weight therefore suggests that the retardation in foetal growth is the cause and not the consequence of the retardation in placental growth. If this conclusion is accepted then the hypothesis of over-crowding in the uterus must be rejected. An additional argument against the overcrowding hypothesis is the fact that the birth weight of dichorial twins does not depend on whether they have a single fused placenta or two separate placentae; for example, it can be calculated from the data of Potter (1963) that the median birth weight of dichorial twins with a fused placenta was 5·27 pounds compared with 5·33 pounds in twins with separate placentae; the difference is negligible. On the hypothesis of overcrowding one would expect a lower birth weight when the twins are implanted close together with a fused placenta than when they are implanted far apart in the uterus with separate placentae.

It therefore seems likely that the retardation in foetal growth is due to undernutrition, either through lack of nutriments or hormones in the blood or through the insufficiency of the blood supply to the uterus. Two lines of evidence suggest that the latter factor is to blame. Morris, Osborn, and Wright (1955) have found that the utero-placental circulation is slower in twin than in single pregnancy, and Walker and Turnbull (1955) have found increased haemoglobin and red cell levels in twins at birth which they interpret as evidence of intra-uterine anoxia.

We must finally consider the reason for the decreased length of gestation in multiple births. The factors which determine the onset of labour are imperfectly understood, but it seems likely that they are largely hormonal. The placenta secretes large amounts both of progesterone which inhibits and of oestrogen which promotes uterine contraction, and the current theory is that during pregnancy progesterone blocks the uterine contractions, but that this blockage is overcome at the end of pregnancy either through increased production of oestrogen or through decreased production of progesterone and that labour then follows. According to this theory the size of the foetus plays no part in determining the onset of labour; it has in fact been shown in Rhesus monkeys that, if the foetus is removed half way through pregnancy but the placenta and membranes are left intact, pregnancy continues for the normal period (about six months) and 'birth' then follows (van Wagenen and Newton 1943). However, it seems likely that uterine distension also plays a subsidiary role in determining the onset of labour since hydramnios, in which the amniotic sac becomes grossly distended with excess fluid, often leads to premature birth (Eastman and Hellmann 1966). The most reasonable hypothesis is that hormonal factors play the leading role in determining the onset of labour, but that mechanical factors, and in particular the degree of distension of the uterus, play a subsidiary role through changing the sensitivity of the uterus to the hormones which control its contraction.

We have already seen that the mean birth weights of singletons, twins, triplets, and quadruplets are about seven, five, four and three pounds respectively, so that the *total* foetal weights at birth are about seven, ten, twelve, and twelve pounds. The most likely explanation of the progressively earlier onset of birth in higher multiple births is that it is due to uterine distension caused by the greater total foetal weight; it may be suggested that the uterus will not, on average, tolerate a total weight greater than about twelve pounds. An interesting fact which supports this theory is that when one twin is present in each horn of a bicornuate uterus (see Chapter 8) the delivery of the second twin may be delayed for several weeks after that of the first twin; it seems likely that the two horns of a divided uterus can react independently of each other, and that when the uterine distension is relieved by the expulsion of one twin pregnancy can continue in the other horn for the natural period of a single pregnancy. However, the possibility cannot be ignored that the early onset of labour in multiple births may be due to a change in hormonal balance caused by the larger amount of placental tissue.

Mortality

Mortality in early life is considerably higher in multiple than in single births. Table 3.4 shows that the stillbirth rate is about

Table 3.4. Stillbirth rate per thousand births (1939–57) and infant mortality per thousand live births (1950) in England and Wales (Registrar-General's Statistical Reviews, Heady and Heasman 1959)

	Single births	Twins	Triplets	Quadruplets
Stillbirth rate	26	58	86	120
Neonatal mortality	16	89	280	
Postneonatal mortality	11	22	(14)†	
Mortality in second year	2·4	2·5		

† Based on four deaths only.

twice as high in twins as in single births, about three times as high in triplets, and four times as high in quadruplets. The differences in neonatal mortality (in the first month of life) are even greater, being about five times as high in twins as in single births, and nearly twenty times as high in triplets. The differential between multiple and single births is less marked in the remainder of the first year of life (the postneonatal period) and has disappeared in the second year of life.

Stillbirth is defined as death of the foetus before it is completely expelled or extracted from its mother; death may occur either before the onset of labour (antepartum death) or during labour (intrapartum death). Among single births antepartum deaths account for rather less than half of all stillbirths (Butler and Bonham 1963) but in twins they form about three-quarters of them (Guttmacher and Kohl 1958). It can be concluded that the increase in the stillbirth rate in multiple births is due to an increase in the frequency of intra-uterine deaths occurring before labour. It seems likely that this increased mortality before birth is due to the same factors which cause the retardation of foetal growth.

Live-born twins are at a double disadvantage compared with single babies since they are not only retarded in growth but

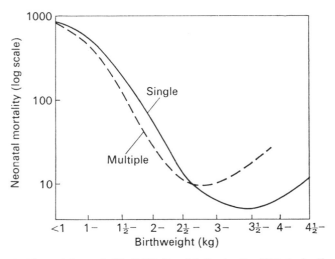

FIG. 3.2. Neonatal mortality/1000 live births in the U.S.A. in the first quarter of 1950, by birth weight. (Redrawn from Montagu (1952).)

they are also born about three weeks early. It is therefore not surprising that infant mortality should be increased to an even greater extent than the stillbirth rate. (Stillborn twins are also born early, but this cannot be regarded as the cause of a death which occurs before the onset of labour.) It is interesting to consider the relationship, shown in Fig. 3.2, between neonatal mortality and birth weight, which is a crude index of the joint effects of retarded growth and early labour. Neonatal mortality declines with increasing birth weight until it reaches a minimum value at about eight pounds in single and seven pounds in multiple births; above this weight mortality rises again. This increase in mortality at high birth weights is independent of the increase in mortality which occurs when gestation is unduly prolonged, since birth weight and length of gestation are uncorrclated when the normal length of gestation is cxcecded. The high mortality of babies who are heavier than average may be due to maternal or placental insufficiency caused by excessive foetal demand, but further research is required on this subject.

It will also be seen from Fig. 3.2 that mortality is lower in multiple than in single births at birth weights under two and a half kilogrammes (five and a half pounds) but is higher at birth weights above this value. Record, Gibson, and McKeown (1952), who obtained similar results in English data, suggested that the higher mortality in single births at low birth weights is due to the fact that single births of five and a half pounds or less are unusual and are likely to have been precipitated by factors such as severe congenital malformations, toxaemia, and placenta praevia which predispose to early death; on the other hand, twins of the same weight are normal and will not be specially associated with foetal and maternal complications which predispose to early death. In support of this view they were able to show that the higher death rate among single births at low birth weights was largely due to the high incidence of foetal and maternal complications among them. The higher mortality in multiple than in single births at birth weights above five and a half pounds is due to the fact that mortality begins to rise with birth weight earlier in multiple than in single pregnancies, presumably because the combined weight of the foetuses places a greater strain on the mother.

Since monochorial twins are more retarded in growth than dichorial twins and suffer the additional hazard of the transfusion syndrome we might expect their mortality to be greater. Table 3.5 shows that this is the case. The death rates among monochorial twins in the last column have been estimated on the assumption that the increase in the death rate among like-sexed twins is entirely due to an increase among monochorial twins and that such twins form about one third of all like-sexed twins. Direct evidence of the increased mortality in monochorial twins has been provided by Naeye, Benirschke, Hagstrom, and Marcus (1966) who show from extensive hospital records that the perinatal mortality is about twice as high in monochorial as in dichorial twins (139 and 66 per thousand respectively), which is in good agreement with the results of Table 3.5. (Perinatal deaths include stillbirths and deaths in the first week

Table 3.5. Stillbirth rate and infant mortality per thousand by sex type of twins, England and Wales, 1950 (Heady and Heasman 1959)

	Unlike-sexed twins	Like-sexed twins	Monochorial twins (estimated)
Stillbirth rate	43	62	100
Neonatal mortality	77	96	128
Postneonatal mortality	23	22	20

of life. It is unfortunate that the bastard word 'perinatal' has become entrenched in the literature instead of the more correct word 'circumnatal'.) It will be seen from Table 3.5 that the increase in mortality in monochorial compared with dichorial twins is proportionately greatest in the stillbirth rate and has disappeared after the first month of life. This is in contrast with the increase in mortality in multiple compared with single births shown in Table 3.4 which is proportionately greatest in the neonatal period. This can be explained by the fact that monochorial twins have an inferior prenatal environment compared with dichorial twins but are not usually born earlier. It seems likely that the transfusion syndrome is the main cause of the increased mortality since among thirty-eight twins with this syndrome diagnosed by Rausen, Seki, and Strauss (1965) there were twenty-one stillbirths, four neonatal deaths, and only eleven surviving infants.

The data in Tables 3.4 and 3.5 only relate to births occurring after the twenty-eighth week of pregnancy. It has been shown by Naeye, Benirschke, Hagstrom, and Marcus (1966) that about four per cent of monochorial and one and a half per cent of

dichorial twin pregnancies terminate between the twenty-fourth
and twenty-seventh weeks of pregnancy; almost none of these
twins survived. Very few single pregnancies terminate in this
period (Stevenson and Warnock 1959). It follows that if Tables
3.4 and 3.5 included all births terminating after, say, the
twentieth week of pregnancy they would show a rather higher
differential mortality between multiple and single births, and
between monochorial and dichorial twins. It is likely that the
increased frequency of monochorial compared with dichorial
twins who are born before the twenty-eighth week is due to
the transfusion syndrome since Rausen, Seki, and Strauss (1965)
found that five out of nineteen cases had a gestational age
between twenty and twenty-seven weeks.

It is rather difficult to obtain reliable information about the
frequency of twin pregnancies which abort before the twentieth
week of gestation, but it does not seem that they are any more
likely to do so than single pregnancies (Benirschke and Driscoll
1967). This impression may be misleading, however, since the
death of one twin in the second or third month of pregnancy,
when most spontaneous abortions occur (Stevenson and
Warnock 1959), may well escape recognition.

Indirect evidence about prenatal mortality is provided by
the sex ratio of multiple births about which data for several
countries are shown in Table 3.6.There is a small but consistent

Table 3.6. The sex ratio in multiple births

Country	Single	Twin	Triplet
England and Wales	0·515	0·508±0·001	0·480±0·009
France	0·514	0·506±0·001	0·471±0·009
Italy	0·515	0·508±0·001	0·487±0·008
U.S.A., White	0·514	0·507±0·001	0·498±0·006
U.S.A., Negro	0·507	0·501±0·001	0·502±0·012
Japan	0·519	0·520±0·004	0·515±0·041

fall in the sex ratio among twins, and a rather larger fall among
triplets, though the latter is less consistent because of the small

numbers on which the figures are based. The well-known racial differences in the sex ratio are also apparent. One possible explanation of these facts is that a female embryo may be more likely to divide than a male embryo to form monozygotic twins and triplets, which would cause a fall in the sex ratio in these multiple births but would leave the sex ratio among dizygotic twins and trizygotic triplets unchanged. This is quite a plausible explanation since monozygotic twinning is aetiologically similar to the congenital abnormalities, among which wide differences in the sex ratio exist. However, three lines of evidence indicate that this is not the correct explanation. Firstly, if the fall in the sex ratio is confined to monozygotic twins, it should be twice as large in Japan, where two thirds of the twins are monozygotic, as in European countries where only about one third of the twins are monozygotic. In fact Japan is the only country in which no fall in the sex ratio has been demonstrated. Secondly, if this hypothesis is correct, the sex ratio should be considerably smaller among like-sexed than among unlike-sexed triplets since all the monozygotic triplets must be like-sexed while three quarters of the trizygotic triplets will be of unlike sex (see Chapter 5). In fact, in the combined data for England and Wales, Italy, and the U.S.A. the sex ratios for like-sexed and unlike-sexed triplets are almost the same (0·491 and 0·494 respectively). Thirdly, an examination of the relationship between the sex ratio of twins and maternal age reveals no significant trend, despite the fact that the proportion of dizygotic twins increases sharply with age.

It can be concluded that the likelihood of monozygotic twinning is independent of the sex of the embryo and that the fall in the sex ratio in multiple births is due to some factor which affects both types of twins and all three types of triplets to a similar extent. It seems likely that this factor is an increased prenatal mortality which is greater for male than for female foetuses, since it is known that in single pregnancies the chance of abortion is greater for male than for female foetuses (Stevenson 1959). Part of the increased prenatal mortality in multiple births is undoubtedly due to premature termination of pregnancy between the twentieth and twenty-eighth weeks of pregnancy rather than to 'true' abortion before the twentieth week, but it is impossible to estimate how much.

Complications of pregnancy

Twins thus experience a greatly increased mortality both before and after birth because of their retarded growth, their premature delivery, and because of the transfusion syndrome in monochorial twins. In addition to these factors they suffer from a higher frequency of abnormalities of pregnancy and birth than single babies. This is not the place to discuss all the complications which may arise in twin pregnancy, nor have I the knowledge to do so, but some mention must be made of the more important of them.

The most important maternal complications of twin pregnancy are toxaemia and hydramnios. Toxaemia is a maternal disorder characterized by high blood pressure, oedema, and the presence of albumen in the urine; if untreated it may lead to convulsions. Its cause is obscure, but according to one theory it is primarily due to the failure of the blood supply of the uterus to keep pace with the demands of the foetus (Swyer 1954). If this theory is correct it is not surprising to find that toxaemia is more common in twin pregnancies. It is rather difficult to measure its incidence exactly, because different criteria have been used to define the disorder, but it seems to occur in about five to ten per cent of single pregnancies, and about three times as often in twin pregnancies (Bender 1952). In single pregnancies perinatal mortality is considerably increased by toxaemia, but this does not seem to be the case in twin pregnancy. According to Bender (1952) 'this was because toxaemia was uncommon in those pregnancies ending before the thirty-third week which contributed most heavily to the foetal mortality. In other words, many of the pregnancies in which the babies were lost did not continue long enough for toxaemia to develop as a complication'.

Hydramnios is the occurrence of an excessive amount of amniotic fluid. The normal quantity of fluid is about one litre, but in hydramnios three or more litres may be present. Its frequency depends on the diagnostic criteria used, but on average it seems to occur in about one per cent of single and in about five per cent of twin pregnancies, although the latter figure should more properly be expressed as two and a half per cent of twin births since it may occur in either twin (Bender 1952, Stevenson 1960). It has been suggested that the increased frequency of hydramnios is confined to monochorial twins and is an expression of the transfusion syndrome, but the evidence is inconclusive; Guttmacher (1939) found no increase in the frequency of monochorial twins in hydramniotic twin pregnancies. Perinatal mortality is greatly increased in hydramnios, largely because of the increased frequency of congenital malformations, in particular anencephaly, but also because of prematurity (Bender 1952, Stevenson 1960). The cause of hydramnios is unknown and much further work remains to be done.

It was once thought that the length of labour was increased in twin pregnancy because of distension of the uterus, but it is now known that this is not the case (Bender 1952). The most important complication of labour in twins is malpresentation. Most babies are born head first (vertex presentation), but it sometimes happens that they are lying with their buttocks first at the beginning of labour (breech presentation) or across the uterus (transverse presentation). Delivery is more difficult in these positions, and it is usually necessary for the obstetrician to assist delivery in some way. Perinatal mortality is greatly increased in breech and transverse presentations, although part of the increase is due not to the method of presentation but to other factors, such as prematurity, which predispose both to abnormal presentation and to early death.

The approximate frequencies of these types of presentation in single and twin births are shown in Table 3.7 together with the perinatal mortality in twins. It will be seen that there is a big increase in the frequencies of breech and transverse presentations in twins, and that the perinatal mortality is about twice as high in breech as in vertex presentations; the numbers were

Table 3.7. Presentation and perinatal mortality in twins (Guttmacher and Kohl 1958)

Presentation	Frequency (per cent)		Perinatal mortality per thousand	
	Single	Twin	First twin	Second twin
Vertex	95	63	84	112
Breech	3	30	176	206
Transverse	$\frac{1}{2}$	$4\frac{1}{2}$		
Other	$1\frac{1}{2}$	$2\frac{1}{2}$		

inadequate to calculate mortalities for other types of presentation. The combinations of the three main types of presentation in 1 212 pairs of twins are shown in Table 3.8, together with

Table 3.8. Presentation of 1 212 pairs of twins and their expected distribution on the assumption of independence (Guttmacher and Kohl 1958)

Presentation	Frequency	Expected frequency
Both vertex	568	557
One vertex, one breech	449	464
Both breech	106	97
One vertex, one transverse	59	65
One breech, one transverse	23	27
Both transverse	7	2

the frequencies predicted on the assumption that the presentation is independently determined in each twin; the agreement with prediction is good, except for an excess of double transverse presentations. However, when the twins present in different positions, their presentation influences the order of birth. When one twin presents in the vertex and the other in the breech position, the twin in the vertex position is delivered first about one and a half times as often as the other twin, and when one twin is longitudinal (either vertex or breech) and the other transverse, the longitudinal twin is delivered first about eight times as often as the transverse twin (Browne and Browne 1960). It is for this reason that perinatal mortality is reported separately for first and second twins in Table 3.7. It seems likely that vertex presentations are the rule in single births partly through gravity, since the head is the heaviest part of the foetus, and partly because the uterus is widest at its top end whereas the foetus is widest at its buttocks. In the highly distended uterus of twin pregnancy, however, it is easier for the foetus to be accommodated in the breech and transverse positions.

It will also be seen from Table 3.7 that mortality is higher in the second than in the first twin. This fact has been denied by some authors, but Wyshak and White (1963) have collected together data on over 12 000 pairs of twins reported in twenty-eight papers and have shown conclusively that there is an increased mortality in the second twin. Furthermore the increase in mortality occurs both in stillbirths and in neonatal deaths: in over 6 000 pairs of twins reported in thirteen papers in which stillbirths and neonatal deaths were reported separately, the stillbirth rates for first and second twins were 34 and 49 per thousand respectively, while the neonatal death rates were 72 and 89 per thousand. There are several reasons for the increased mortality of the second twin. Firstly, when one twin dies in the uterus before birth (such twins are usually recognisable as macerated foetuses), there is a tendency for the living twin to be born first (MacDonald 1962, Potter 1961, Benirschke and Driscoll 1967, Butler and Alberman 1969). Secondly, when twins are lying in different positions in the uterus there is a tendency for the twin in the normal, vertex position to be born first. Thirdly, the second twin probably suffers a greater risk of anoxia because of the increased length of labour and because of the possibility that the placenta may separate after the birth of the first twin. On the other side of the balance sheet is the fact that the first twin probably has a greater risk of birth injury since it must dilate the cervix whereas the second twin passes through an already dilated cervix. It is not possible to separate the effects of these different factors with the data at present available.

Post-natal development

We have seen that the retarded foetal growth and early delivery of twins play a large part in determining their increased mortality, and it is of interest to consider whether twins who survive are in any way affected by these factors. It has also been suggested that the fact of being brought up together as twins may have an effect on the development of their intelligence and personality. We must therefore discuss briefly whether there are any differences in the physical and mental development of twins and singletons after birth.

In an important longitudinal study Drillien (1964) has shown that at birth there is a difference of about two and a half inches in height between babies weighing under four and a half pounds and those weighing over five and a half pounds; this difference is still present at five years of age but has been reduced to about one and a half inches. There was no difference in height at any age between twins and singletons of the same birth weight, but the difference in birth weight has led to a difference in height between five-year-old twins and singletons of just under an inch. Most of this difference persists since Husen (1959) found that Swedish male twins called up for army service are about half an inch in height below the average. It can also be calculated from Drillien's data that five-year-old twins are about three pounds lighter in weight than singletons.

It can be concluded that the retarded foetal growth of twins has a small but lasting effect on their post-natal physical development. Of far greater importance, however, is the increased risk of gross physical or mental handicap. Infants of low birth weight have an increased risk of such handicap, particularly if their birth weight is less than about five pounds.

Thus Drillien (1968) found that at seven years of age about twenty per cent of children with birth weights between three and a half and four and a half pounds were moderately or severely handicapped, whilst this frequency rose to over fifty per cent for children whose birth weight was less than three and a quarter pounds. Children classified as moderately or severely handicapped were ineducable or required special educational provision on account of physical defect or mental retardation or attended ordinary school but suffered from cerebral palsy and/ or epilepsy. The frequency of handicap was about the same in single and twin children of the same birth weight, but the overall frequency of handicapped children must be higher in twins because of their lower birth weight. This fact has been confirmed in several investigations. Thus Berg and Kirman (1960) found 75 twins among 1 390 mentally defective patients, representing a frequency of 5·4 per cent, compared with an expected frequency of about 2·0 per cent in the general population after allowing for stillbirths and infant deaths. Similarly Illingworth and Woods (1960) found 23 twins among 593 mentally retarded children, which represents a frequency of 3·9 per cent, while Allen and Kallmann (1955) found a rather lower frequency of 3·1 per cent in New York, but even this figure is considerably higher than the frequency of twins in the general population.

It can be concluded that twins are about twice as likely as singletons to be mentally defective. In the case of cerebral palsy, in which low birth weight is particularly implicated, the frequency of twins is even higher. In an extensive investigation in Denmark Hanson (1960) found 161 twins among 2 389 cases of cerebral palsy, giving a frequency of 6·7 per cent, which is over three times the population frequency. Similar results have been found by other authors (Russell 1961, Illingworth and Woods 1960, Asher and Schonell 1950, Greenspan and Deaver 1953, Yue 1955).

The increased incidence of congenital malformations in mono-zygotic but not in dizygotic twins has already been discussed in the last chapter.

We turn now to the possible effects on intelligence and personality which may be produced by the fact of having a twin brother or sister. It has been shown by Day (1932) and Davis (1941) that twins are retarded in speech development compared with singletons of the same age, sex, and social class. This retardation is probably due to the fact that mothers of twins have less time to devote to them than she would have for a singleton and may be inclined to leave them to play by themselves; in consequence twins have less contact with adults and may even develop a sort of private language only understood by themselves. It is known that the development of speech is markedly affected by the degree of contact with adults; thus only children show a striking superiority in language development, and children from institutions a marked retardation (Nisbet 1953).

It has been shown in several investigations that twins are on average less intelligent than singletons by about five IQ points (Byrns and Healy 1936, Husen 1953, Mehrotra and Maxwell 1949, Sandon 1957, Tabah and Sutter 1954). It seems likely that most if not all of this deficit is due either to their retarded speech development or to the same factors which cause this retardation. It is known that increasing family size has an adverse effect on intelligence, as does a short interval between births (Tabah and Sutter 1954), probably because the children receive less individual attention from their parents. These two factors are sufficient to account for the lower intelligence of twins since they belong, on average, to larger families (including themselves) than singletons and are born simultaneously. It is therefore suggested that the increased frequency of gross mental retardation in twins is due to their retarded foetal growth and premature delivery, but that the slightly lower intelligence of normal twins is due to differences in their upbringing.

It has also been suggested that twins may differ in personality from singletons, but there is little reliable evidence to support this view. It has been shown that twins are no more likely than anyone else to develop psychiatric disorders (Slater and Shields

1953, Shields 1954), and it can be concluded that the effect of twinning on personality is probably small. As Shields (1954) remarks, 'being a twin may be of much the same kind of importance as being an only child or being the eldest or the youngest of a family'. Zazzo (1960) has suggested that twins are more timid and are less likely to marry than singletons, but confirmation of his findings is required.

Finally, some mention must be made of the suspicion that monozygotic twins are frequently 'mirror images' of one another; for example, one twin may be left-handed and the other right-handed, or one twin may have his internal organs on the wrong side of the body (*situs inversus viscerum*). It was at one time believed that mirror-imaging was caused by division of the embryo after its left and right sides had been established, but recent evidence shows that it does not occur more frequently than would be expected by chance. (See Husen (1959) and Zazzo (1960) for handedness, and Torgersen (1950) for *situs inversus*.)

4 *The Frequency of Twins*

IN this chapter we shall consider the various factors, such as age, race, and nutritional state, which determine the frequency with which twins are born. In order to distinguish between monozygotic and dizygotic twinning, which differ completely in their response to these factors, most authors have relied on Weinberg's method, based on the numbers of twins of like and of unlike sex. This method has already been used in previous chapters, but it now seems appropriate to evaluate its use more critically since it will be employed so extensively in the rest of the chapter.

Measuring the twinning rate

If a pair of twins differs in a single inherited character, such as sex, eye colour, or blood group, they must be dizygotic. On the other hand, a pair of twins can never be proved with certainty to be monozygotic (except by skin grafting) since dizygotic twins could agree in a large number of characters by chance; as the number of concordant characters increases, however, the probability that the twins are monozygotic becomes very high (see the Appendix to Chapter 1). In order to make a diagnosis of zygosity with reasonable accuracy it is thus necessary to investigate a large number of genetic characters or to do a skin graft. It is, however, obviously impossible to pursue such detailed investigations on a large group of twins, particularly at birth; it is also impossible to determine zygosity by physical resemblance at birth. Another method of diagnosis must therefore be found in a statistical study of the frequencies of monozygotic and dizygotic twin births.

It was once the practice of obstetricians to make a diagnosis of zygosity on the evidence of the after-birth, on the assumption that monochorial twins must be monozygotic and that dichorial twins must be dizygotic. However, it has been shown in Chapter 2 that the second part of this assumption is incorrect since monozygotic twins may be either monochorial or dichorial; this method will therefore overestimate the frequency of dizygotic twins. The only reliable method of diagnosis in large numbers of twins is the so-called 'differential method' which was first systematically used by Weinberg in 1901; this method had been known to M. Bertillon as early as 1874 but had been rejected by him because it appeared to give too high a frequency of monozygotic twins compared with estimates made from the evidence of the after-birth. It took some time before it became generally accepted that the evidence of the after-birth was misleading and that Weinberg's method was correct.

To apply Weinberg's method, all that need be known are the numbers of twin maternities of like and of unlike sex. All the monozygotic twins will of course be like-sexed; on the other hand, if equal numbers of boys and girls are born, half the dizygotic twins should be like-sexed and half of unlike sex. Consequently the number of dizygotic twins can be estimated by doubling the number of unlike-sexed twins and the number of monozygotic twins by the difference between the numbers of like-sexed and of unlike-sexed twins. Thus if L and U are the numbers of like-sexed and unlike-sexed twin maternities in a total sample of N maternities, the monozygotic and dizygotic twinning rates are estimated as:

$$m = \frac{(L-U)}{N}$$

and

$$d = \frac{2U}{N}$$

respectively. For example, out of a total of 791 584 maternities in England and Wales in 1960 there were 9 086 twin maternities of which 5 894 were like-sexed (either two boys or two girls) and 3 192 unlike-sexed (one boy and one girl). The monozygotic and dizygotic twinning rates are estimated as:

$$m = (5894 - 3192)/791\ 584 = 0\cdot0034$$

$$d = 2 \times 3192/791\ 584 = 0\cdot0081$$

In practice it is often more convenient to express these figures as twinning rates per thousand maternities, that is to say as 3·4 per thousand and 8·1 per thousand respectively. It should be noted that these rates are based on the numbers of maternities, not of births. It should also be noted that they include stillbirths as well as livebirths.

This method is based on the assumption that the sex ratio is $\frac{1}{2}$ and it might seem desirable to make a correction for the fact that this is not exactly true. The necessary correction is however so small that it can be ignored. If the probability of a male birth is P, then the probability that dizygotic twins will be of the same sex, either both boys or both girls, is $P^2 + (1-P)^2$ and the probability that they will be of different sexes is $2P(1-P)$. If we write $P = \frac{1}{2}+e$, where e is the deviation of the sex ratio from $\frac{1}{2}$, then these probabilities can be rewritten as $\frac{1}{2}+2e^2$ and $\frac{1}{2}-2e^2$ respectively. If e is small, then $2e^2$ will be negligible. For example, if $P = 0\cdot514$, a fairly typical value for the sex ratio, then $e = 0\cdot014$, $2e^2 = 0\cdot0004$, and the probability that dizygotic twins will be like-sexed is $0\cdot5004$ instead of $0\cdot5$; so small a discrepancy can be safely ignored.

It has also been assumed that the sexes of the two twins are determined independently and with the same probability in all parents. Part of the preponderance of like-sexed twins could be explained by supposing that sometimes boys are much more likely to be conceived than girls and that on other occasions the opposite is true. Although there are slight variations in the sex ratio depending on factors such as the age of the parents, no variation has ever been demonstrated of sufficient magnitude to cause an appreciable distortion in Weinberg's method.

Finally, the effect of pre-natal loss has been ignored. It is clear that, if data on twin births are used, including if possible both live and stillbirths, then Weinberg's method estimates the frequencies of monozygotic and dizygotic twins *at birth*. These will probably be less than the corresponding frequencies at conception (or shortly after conception in the case of mono-zygotic twins) because of differential prenatal loss before the twenty-eighth week of pregnancy when births become registrable. Similarly, the frequency of twins in the adult population will be less than their frequency at birth because of their high mortality in the first year of life; furthermore, mortality is higher in monozygotic than in dizygotic twins, so that the relative frequency of monozygotic compared with dizygotic twins will be less in the adult population than at birth. These facts have already been discussed in previous chapters. Unfortunately Renkonen (1967) draws from them the mistaken conclusion that Weinberg's method is defective. If Weinberg's method is applied to data on births it will give unbiased estimates of the frequencies of monozygotic and dizygotic twins *at birth*, provided that prenatal loss is the same among unlike-sexed and like-sexed dizygotic twins, thus maintaining their numerical equality; this assumption seems very plausible. It is not a defect of the method that these frequencies differ from the corresponding frequencies in the adult population.

The approximate equality of like-sexed and unlike-sexed dizygotic twins has been confirmed empirically in sheep. It is known that nearly all sheep twins are dizygotic since two corpora lutea are almost always found, although monozygotic twins do occur very rarely (Henning 1937, 1939, Rae 1956). In an extensive survey Johansson and Hansson (1943) reported 12 076 like-sexed and 12 359 unlike-sexed sheep twins (Rae 1956). In human twins where zygosity has been determined by blood grouping it has been confirmed by Potter (1963) that Weinberg's method is essentially correct.

There is thus good reason to suppose that Weinberg's method provides unbiased estimates of the monozygotic and dizygotic twinning rates at birth, provided of course that the original data are unbiased. It must be remembered, however, that these estimates are subject to random sampling error and may differ considerably from the true twinning rates when the number of observations is small. Because twinning is a rather uncommon event the numbers of like-sexed and unlike-sexed twins in a fixed number of maternities will, to a good approximation, follow the Poisson distribution whose variance is equal to its mean. By the ordinary rules for computing variances we therefore find that:

$$V(m) = \frac{V(L-U)}{N^2} \doteq \frac{(L+U)}{N^2} = \frac{(m+d)}{N}$$

$$V(d) = \frac{4V(U)}{N^2} \doteq \frac{4U}{N^2} = \frac{2d}{N}.$$

The standard errors of m and d are of course found by taking the square roots of the variances, and must then be multiplied by a thousand if the rates are expressed as rates per thousand maternities. It should be observed that the sampling variance of m is proportional to the *total* twinning rate, which means that the monozygotic twinning rate is difficult to measure accurately by this method if monozygotic twins form only a small proportion of all twins. It should also be observed that m and d are negatively correlated since the number of unlike-sexed twins occurs in the formulae for both of them but with a different sign. This negative correlation means that m is likely to be an overestimate of the true value when d is an underestimate, and vice versa.

In interpreting twinning rates it is also necessary to bear in mind the possibility of bias. There are two main sources of data for estimating twinning rates by Weinberg's method, national birth statistics obtained from birth registration records, and maternity hospital records. These figures should not be accepted uncritically if there is any reason to doubt their reliability. There is a tendency for twinning rates based on national birth statistics to be too low due to under-reporting of twins, and for rates based on hospital figures to be too high owing to preferential admission of women with twin pregnancies. This tendency is illustrated in Table 4.1, which shows Japanese

Table 4.1. The twinning rate per thousand in Japan

Source of data	Mono-zygotic	Dizygotic	Mono-/Dizygotic	Reference
Birth statistics, 1923–33	2·1	1·3	1·6	Komai and Fukuoka 1936
Hosp. records, pre-war	7·0	3·8	1·8	Komai and Fukuoka 1936
Midwives' records, 1926–31	3·8	2·7	1·4	Komai and Fukuoka 1936
Birth statistics, 1956	4·1	2·3	1·8	Bulmer 1960b

twinning rates based on (a) pre-war national birth statistics, (b) pre-war hospital records, (c) pre-war midwives' records, and (d) post-war national birth statistics. It will be seen that the ratio of the monozygotic to the dizygotic twinning rates is nearly constant, but that the rates themselves vary widely. Komai and Fukuoka (1936), who collected the pre-war data, considered that the midwives' records were probably reliable, but that the national birth statistics were under-reported, and the hospital records biased in the other direction due to preferential admission of mothers with twins. This supposition is confirmed by the post-war national birth statistics (Bulmer 1960b), which are known to be more reliable than the pre-war statistics, and which are nearly the same as the pre-war midwives' records.

It can be stated in general that in reliable data the dizygotic twinning rate may vary widely under different circumstances but that the monozygotic twinning rate is remarkably constant and usually lies between three and a half and four per thousand; if it lies outside this range there is presumptive evidence for suspecting the data. This cannot of course be taken as an inflexible rule since the reasoning would become circular, but it provides a reliable guide in practice.

Maternal age and parity

As early as 1865 the Scottish physician Matthews Duncan had shown that the relative frequency of twins increased both with the age of the mother and independently with the number of children she had previously borne, usually called her parity; it was later shown by Weinberg (1901) that this increase is almost entirely confined to the dizygotic component of the twinning rate. These facts have subsequently been confirmed by many authors. To demonstrate them here I shall rely mainly on Italian birth statistics for the period 1949–54 which are presented in unusual detail giving a simultaneous breakdown of twin births by sex type, by maternal age in single years, and by parity (Bulmer 1959a). We shall first consider the monozygotic twinning rate.

The relationship between the monozygotic twinning rate and maternal age in Italy is shown in Fig. 4.1; the original data have been combined into three-year age periods in order to reduce the sampling variation. It will be seen that there is a small but consistent increase in the monozygotic twinning rate with the age of the mother, from about three and a half per thousand in young mothers to about four per thousand in older mothers. Table 4.2 shows that this trend is confirmed by data from other countries.

Since maternal age and parity are highly correlated it is necessary to remove the effect of maternal age by some method of standardization in order to see whether there is an independent effect of parity. Fig. 4.2 shows the relationship between the monozygotic twinning rate and parity, after standardization

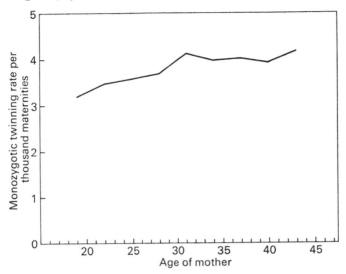

FIG. 4.1. The monozygotic twinning rate by age of mother (Italy, 1949–54).

for maternal age by the direct method (Hill 1966). It can be concluded that parity has little or no effect on the monozygotic twinning rate.

It was argued in Chapter 2 that the causes of monozygotic twinning are similar to those of the congenital malformations, and it is therefore of interest to compare the effects of maternal age and parity on the monozygotic twinning rate with their

Table 4.2. *The relationship between the monozygotic twinning rate and maternal age*

Country	Age of mother			Reference
	Under 25	25–35	Over 35	
Denmark, 1896–1910	3·6	3·8	4·4	Gedda 1951
France, 1902–10	3·0	3·4	3·6	Gedda 1951
France, 1920–49	3·3	3·6	3·9	Bulmer 1958a
England and Wales, 1938–55	3·4	3·5	3·8	Bulmer 1958a
U.S.A. (White), 1938	3·6	3·8	4·3	Bulmer 1958a

effects on the incidence of congenital malformations. In a
review of the latter subject McKeown (1961) has shown, firstly,
that the incidence of most (though not all) congenital malformations increases slightly with maternal age from about ten
per cent less than the average incidence in mothers under

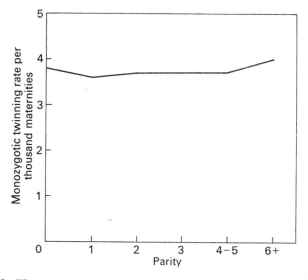

Fig. 4.2. The monozygotic twinning rate by parity, standardized for
maternal age (Italy, 1949–54).

twenty-five to about ten per cent more than the average
incidence in mothers over thirty-five; and, secondly, that the
incidence of most malformations is highest in first pregnancies
(it may be as much as forty per cent higher than the average),
drops sharply to a minimum in second and third pregnancies,
and then either remains constant or begins to increase again in
fourth and subsequent pregnancies. (The effects of parity were
standardized for maternal age, and vice versa.) The stillbirth
rate shows a similar pattern (Morris and Heady 1955). These
facts suggest that the intra-uterine environment is less
favourable in older than in younger mothers, parity being held

constant, due to ageing, and that it is less favourable in primi-
parae than in multiparae, age being held constant, due to the
beneficial usage effect of the first pregnancy.

The monozygotic twinning rate shows the expected slight

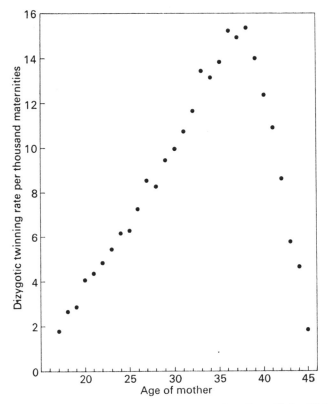

FIG. 4.3. The dizygotic twinning rate by age of mother (Italy, 1949–54).

increase with maternal age, but fails to show any effect of parity.
The main distinction between monozygotic twinning and the
congenital malformations is that twinning occurs at a much
earlier stage of foetal development, at about the time when the
embryo is becoming implanted. It may therefore be suggested
that the adverse effect of maternal age acts throughout the
whole period of foetal life, but that the adverse effect of

primiparity acts only in the later stages after implantation,
and so does not influence monozygotic twinning.

We shall now consider the effects of age and parity on
dizygotic twinning. The relationship between the dizygotic
twinning rate and maternal age in Italy is shown in Fig. 4.3.
It will be seen that the rate rises from nearly zero at puberty

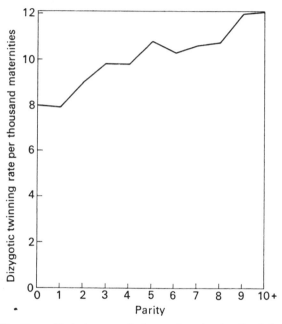

FIG. 4.4. The dizygotic twinnng rate by parity, standardized for maternal
age (Italy, 1949–54).

to a maximum at about thirty-seven, and then falls abruptly
again to zero at the menopause. Fig. 4.4 shows the relationship
between the dizygotic twinning rate and parity, after standardization for maternal age by the direct method; there is a clear
increase in the rate with parity, though the effect is smaller
than that of age. Finally, Fig. 4.5 shows a breakdown of the
dizygotic twinning rate simultaneously by maternal age and
parity; the data have been grouped into three-yearly age groups

and into three parity groups, and rates based on less than 15 000
maternities have been omitted, in order to minimize sampling

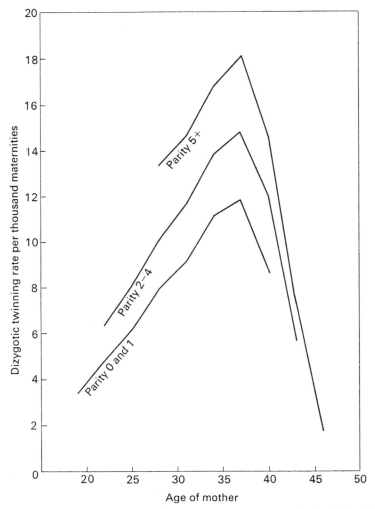

FIG. 4.5. The dizygotic twinning rate by age and parity (Italy, 1949–54.)

errors. The general relationship between the dizygotic twinning
rate and maternal age at each parity level is the same as in
Fig. 4.3, which ignores parity, but the curve is shifted upwards

as the parity increases. The relationship between the dizygotic twinning rate and maternal age has been confirmed in many other countries, but few countries publish data suitable for analysing the effect of parity.

It was suggested in Chapter 2 that the secretion of pituitary gonadotrophin is the main factor which controls the dizygotic

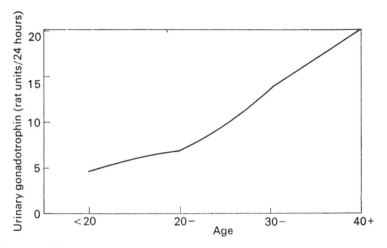

Fig. 4.6. Mean excretion of gonadotrophin in adult, pre-menopausal, women. (Albert *et al.*, 1956.)

twinning rate. In trying to explain the relationship between the dizygotic twinning rate and maternal age it is therefore natural to ask whether the gonadotrophin level varies with age. Gonadotrophins are first detectable at the beginning of adolescence, and it seems likely that the changes associated with adolescence are initiated by the secretion of gonadotrophin, which is itself under the control of the brain (Tanner 1962). In adult, pre-menopausal women Albert, Randall, Smith, and Johnson (1956) have shown that the excretion of gonadotrophin increases with age from about five rat units per day in the under-twenty age group to twenty rat units per day in the over-forty age group; their results are shown in Fig. 4.6. After the menopause the excretion of gonadotrophin increases sharply to about fifty rat units per day, probably due to the release of the pituitary from inhibition by ovarian hormones.

The increase in the dizygotic twinning rate from zero at the menarche to a maximum at about age thirty-seven may therefore be due to increasing secretion of gonadotrophin. The sharp fall in the dizygotic twinning rate from its maximum at thirty-seven back to zero at the meopause is probably a consequence of failing ovarian function as the menopause approaches. The menopause itself is caused by the cessation of ovarian function when the ovaries run out of follicles and it is not unreasonable to suppose that it is preceded by a period of waning ovarian function when the ovaries are unable to respond fully to gonadotrophic stimulation because they are beginning to run short of follicles.

The mechanism of the increase in the dizygotic twinning rate with parity is unknown, but it is not difficult to imagine how the hormonal changes which occur in pregnancy might cause a permanent change in the activity of the pituitary or the ovary; it has in fact been suggested by Loraine (1963) that the increased secretion of gonadotrophin is primarily determined by parity rather than by age, which would invalidate the explanation of the increase of dizygotic twinning with age. It seems to be a general rule in mammals that the average litter size increases with the number of previous litters independently of maternal age. For example, in virgin mice which were allowed to breed for the first time at the age of ten to twelve months, the average number of corpora lutea was 9·5 and the average litter size 5·7; the corresponding figures for mice of the same age which had borne four to six litters previously were 11·2 and 7·1 (Nishimura and Shikata 1960). Similar results have been found in pigs and rats (Hammond 1961). Average litter size also increases with the age of the mother in most mammals, but it usually rises from a low value at puberty to a level plateau which is maintained as long as reproduction continues, rather than rising continuously to a peak and then falling as it does in man. This difference may be connected with the fact that a well-defined menopause does not seem to occur except in man.

The age of the father has so far been ignored in this discussion although it is possible that it may have an effect on the twinning rate. Tables of twin maternities broken down simultaneously by age of mother and father are available for the U.S.A., Egypt, and New Zealand. After standardization for maternal maternal age there is a small but definite increase in the twinning rate with father's age in the first two countries but not in New Zealand (Bulmer 1959a). Part at least of the increase with father's age in the first two countries is probably an indirect expression of the increase in the twinning rate with parity since wives whose husbands are older than themselves will, on the average, have been married longer, and so have had more children, than wives of the same age whose husbands are younger than themselves. It is thus doubtful to what extent the age of the father has a direct biological effect on the twinning rate, but it seems safe to conclude that it is small if it exists at all. There is certainly no evidence that the frequency of dizygotic twinning decreases as the age of the father increases, as would be predicted on the theory that the frequency with which two ova are both fertilized is dependent on the quality or quantity of the sperm.

Another rather curious finding is that there is a higher twinning rate among women who conceive in the first three months of marriage than among women who do not conceive until later (Bulmer 1959a). There are several possible explanations of this fact, one of which is that it may be due to superfecundation (see p. 18). Unfortunately nothing is known about the frequency of double ovulation, but it seems quite likely that sometimes only one of the two ova released may be fertilized; if coitus occurs again fairly soon the other ovum may be fertilized and may thus lead to the production of dizygotic twins through superfecundation. If this were the case one would expect to find a higher frequency of dizygotic twinning in couples who have very frequent intercourse. The higher twinning rate among women who conceive in the first few months of marriage might therefore result either from a high frequency of intercourse at that time or from the fact that couples who have intercourse frequently are more likely to conceive quickly. Another possibly related finding is that, after standardization for maternal age, the twinning rate is higher in unmarried than in married mothers in Scandinavia (Eriksson and Fellman 1961).

Racial differences

The human species is divided by anthropologists into three great racial groups, the Caucasoids, the Negroids, and the Mongoloids, which correspond roughly with the white, black, and yellow races of popular nomenclature. The Caucasoid race, which is the most diverse of the three and which is characterized by white or brown skin and by straight or wavy hair, comprises the inhabitants of Europe, of Africa north of the Sahara, of Southwest Asia, and of most of India, together with emigrants from these places to other parts of the globe, particularly America. The Negroid race, characterized by black, woolly hair, black skin, thick, out-turned lips, and protruding jaw, has its home in Africa south of the Sahara. The Mongoloid race, characterized by dark, straight hair, yellow skin, broad head, and an epicanthic eye-fold, has its home in Eastern Asia with off-shoots among the American Indians and the Eskimos. There are also a few minor groups, such as the Australian aborigines, but nearly all the inhabitants of the world belong to one of the three major racial groups.

The monozygotic twinning rate is nearly constant at about three and a half per thousand in all races. The dizygotic twinning rate, on the other hand, varies widely; as a broad generalization it can be stated that the dizygotic twinning rate is about eight per thousand in Caucasoids, about twice as large in Negroes, and less than half as large in Mongoloids. There are also smaller variations within these racial groups. We shall now consider the available data in detail.

Reliable and extensive population statistics are available on the twinning rate in many European countries. Some recent figures are shown in Table 4.3. They are arranged in ascending order of the dizygotic twinning rate and they have all been standardized for maternal age. It will be seen that the monozygotic twinning rate is about three and a half per thousand in

Table 4.3. The twinning rate in Europe, standardized for maternal age
(Bulmer 1960b)

Country	Period	Dizygotic	Monozygotic
Spain	1951–53	5·9	3·2
Portugal	1955–56	6·5	3·6
France	1946–51	7·1	3·7
Belgium	1950	7·3	3·6
Austria	1952–56	7·5	3·4
Luxembourg	1901–53	7·9	3·5
Switzerland	1943–48	8·1	3·6
Holland	1946–55	8·1	3·7
West Germany	1950–55	8·2	3·3
Norway	1946–54	8·3	3·8
Sweden	1946–55	8·6	3·2
Italy	1949–55	8·6	3·7
England and Wales	1946–55	8·9	3·6
East Germany	1950–55	9·1	3·3

all countries, and that the dizygotic twinning rate has a typical value of about eight per thousand, with a centre of rather low values in south-west Europe.

In view of the low dizygotic twinning rate in the Iberian peninsula it is of interest to examine the geographical distribution of the twinning rate in the neighbouring country of France in detail. Fig. 4.7 shows the distribution of the dizygotic twinning rate in the ninety departments of France. It will be seen that the rate is low in the south-west near the Iberian border and gradually increases as we move towards the north-east. There are also two isolated areas of rather high twinning rate in the Massif Central and in Brittany. The latter is particularly interesting since there is good reason to suppose that the

Bretons are ethnically distinct from the rest of France. The area of high twinning rate in this part of France coincides almost exactly with the area of high B blood-group frequency found by Vallois (1949). In particular, the only department in

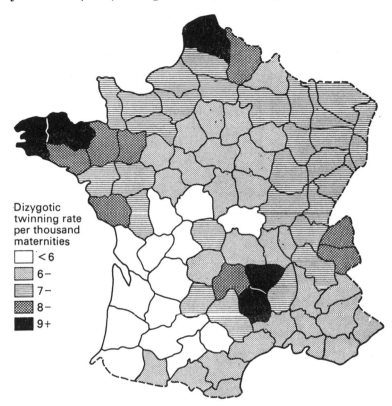

Dizygotic
twinning rate
per thousand
maternities

☐ <6
▨ 6–
▤ 7–
▨ 8–
■ 9+

FIG. 4.7. The distribution of the dizygotic twinning rate in France (Bulmer, 1960b).

Brittany in which the dizygotic twinning rate is less than eight per thousand is Loire-Inferieure. Vallois found that this was the Breton department with the lowest frequency of the B blood group, which he attributed to the fact that the Loire is the natural route for immigration into Brittany so that the population of this department is most likely to be of mixed ancestry; it also contains Nantes, the largest city in Brittany and the most likely to attract immigrants from elsewhere in France. There is thus good evidence that the high dizygotic twinning rate in Brittany is a reflection of an ethnic difference. But compared with the rest of Europe the twinning rate in Brittany is normal and the rate elsewhere in France is low. It

Table 4.4. The twinning rate in India and Pakistan, based on hospital figures

City	Monozygotic	Dizygotic	Number of twins
Ahmedabad	5·3	7·6	225
Bangalore	2·9	7·3	493
Baroda	2·5	6·2	118
Bombay	4·3	6·8	1 643
Bombay†	5·0	7·2	490
Calcutta	3·3	8·1	876
Calcutta†	2·8	11·0	268
Dibrugarh	3·5	7·0	105
Hyberabad	5·0	7·9	258
Lahore	7·8	15·5	108
Lucknow	5·2	8·0	109
Nagpur	6·4	11·1	164
Patna	6·2	11·2	115
Trivandrum	7·9	9·0	278
Visakhapatnam	4·7	8·5	361
Total	4·3	7·8	5 611

† Stevenson, Johnston, Stewart, and Golding (1966).

therefore seems reasonable to conclude that the low twinning rate in Spain, Portugal and south-west France reflects an ethnic distinction of the population of that area. It is possible that this fact has an explanation in terms of the migrations of peoples in prehistory, but at the moment this remains a matter of speculation.

The Indians form the second great sub-group of the Caucasoid race. Unfortunately no Indian population birth statistics are available, but Table 4.4 shows twinning rates based on hospital records throughout India and Pakistan. All the figures were sent to me through the kindness of the medical staff of the hospitals concerned, to whom I here record my gratitude, with the exception of the additional sets of figures for Bombay and Calcutta, which are quoted from Stevenson, Johnston, Stewart, and Golding (1966). In interpreting these figures it must be remembered first that many of them are based on rather small numbers, secondly that they have not been standardized for maternal age, and thirdly that they are liable to inflationary bias since they are based on hospital deliveries. The degree of bias may well vary from one hospital to another depending on their criteria of admission of pregnant women; it seems likely, for example, that the bias is exceptionally large in Lahore since both the monozygotic and the dizygotic rates are nearly twice the average. In the light of these considerations the twinning rates seem to be fairly homogeneous throughout the area. The overall monozygotic and dizygotic rates are 4·3 and and 7·8 per thousand respectively. The monozygotic rate is not much higher than normal and it therefore seems likely that the bias in these figures is, on the average, small. It can be concluded that the dizygotic twinning rate for Indians lies at the lower end of the European range.

We turn next to the negro race. It has been known for some time that the twinning rate is higher in American negroes than in white Americans. This is shown graphically in Fig. 4.8, from which it will be seen that the dizygotic twinning rate is about one and a half times as large in negroes as in whites at all maternal ages; there is no consistent difference in the monozygotic rates. There is considerable mixture of white blood in American negroes and one might therefore expect that the dizygotic twinning rate would be even higher in pure-blooded African negroes.

A number of African hospital twinning rates have been published and are summarized in Table 4.5. The same reservations must be made in interpreting these figures as for the Indian figures; in particular the sample size is in many cases very small. It is clear, however, that the dizygotic twinning rate

7

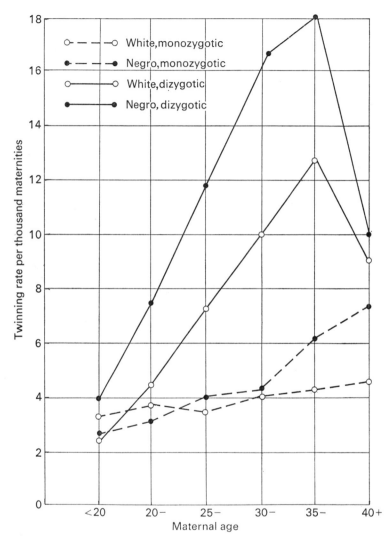

FIG. 4.8. The twinning rate among American whites and negroes, by maternal age (Bulmer, 1958a).

is high. Furthermore, the dizygotic twinning rate among the Bantu-speaking peoples of Central and Southern Africa seems to be fairly constant at a value of about twenty per thousand.

Table 4.5. The twinning rate in Africa, based on hospital figures

Area	Tribe	Monozygotic	Dizygotic	No. of twins	Reference
BANTU					
Transvaal	Swazi	4	24	28	Jeffreys 1953
Natal	Zulu	7	21	116	Jeffreys 1953
Zululand	Zulu	1	21	92	Bulmer 1960b
N. Transvaal	Shangaan	9	32	41	Jeffreys 1953
N. Transvaal	Xosa	0	27	29	Jeffreys 1953
Bechuanaland	Tswana	8	10	87	Jeffreys 1953
Johannesburg		4	16	710	Jeffreys 1953
Johannesburg		5	22	290	Bulmer 1960b
Durban		2	21	66	Jeffreys 1953
Pretoria		3	17	197	Stevenson et al. 1966
Cape Town	'Cape coloured'	8	5	40	Stevenson et al. 1966
S. Rhodesia	Mashona	2	27	100	Ross 1952
Leopoldville		3	19	500	Bulmer 1960b
Elisabethville		4	13	270	Bulmer 1960b
Tanganyika	Hangaza	4	20	39	Roberts 1964
WEST AFRICA NORTH OF THE BANTU LINE					
Br. Camerons	Banso	3	13	72	Jeffreys 1953
E. Nigeria	Ibo	10	23	109	Cox 1963
S. Nigeria	Ibo	5	22	90	Jeffreys 1953
Ibadan, Nigeria	Yoruba	5	40	603	Bulmer 1960b
Ilesha, W. Nigeria	Yoruba	5	49	158	Knox and Morley 1960
Igbo-Ora, W. Nigeria	Yoruba	4	42	177	Nylander 1969 (All births)
Kano, N. Nigeria	Hausa	5	10	44	Jeffreys 1953
Gambia		7	10	57	Bulmer 1960b

The low rate among the 'Cape coloured' population of Cape Town is an exception which proves the rule since these people are largely of Malay origin (Stevenson, Johnston, Stewart, and Golding 1966). North of the Bantu line the rates are more variable. The astonishingly high rate among the Yoruba of

Nigeria is probably genuine, since it has been independently reported from two hospitals, and since the figure obtained by myself is based on quite a large sample of 'booked' cases only, emergency cases having been excluded; maternity beds are so short in Africa that a bed must be booked at a very early stage

Table 4.6. The twinning rate in Asia

Ethnic group	Mono-zygotic	Dizy-gotic	$\dfrac{\text{Dizygotic}}{\text{Monozygotic}}$	Source	Reference
Japanese	2·1	1·3	0·6	Birth statistics, pre-war	Komai and Fukuoka 1936
,,	7·0	3·8	0·6	Hospital records	Komai and Fukuoka 1936
,,	3·8	2·7	0·7	Midwives' records	Komai and Fukuoka 1936
,,	4·1	2·3	0·6	Birth statistics, 1956	Bulmer 1960b
,,	5·3	2·2	0·4	Birth statistics, Hawaii, post-war	Morton, Chung, and Mi 1967
Chinese	2·0	1·4	0·7	Birth statistics, Formosa, pre-war	Komai and Fukuoka 1936
,,	6·6	4·1	0·6	Hospital records, Singapore	Millis 1959b
,,	4·8	2·8	0·6	Hospital records, Malaya	Stevenson et al. 1966
,,	5·7	6·8	1·2	Hospital records, Hong Kong	Stevenson et al. 1966
,,	6·1	2·1	0·3	Birth statistics, Hawaii, post-war	Morton et al. 1967
Koreans	6·7	5·8	0·8	Hospital records	Komai and Fukuoka 1936
,,	5·9	7·9	1·3	Hospital records	Kang and Cho 1962
,,	3·6	5·1	1·4	Interview of mothers	Kang and Cho 1962
Malay	7·7	5·2	0·7	Hospital records, Malaya	Stevenson et al. 1966
,,	7·7	2·7	0·4	Hospital records, Manila	Stevenson et al. 1966
,,	3·0	2.2	0·7	Birth statistics, Hawaii, post-war	Morton et al. 1967
Hawaiian	3·7	3·9	1·1	Birth statistics, Hawaii, post-war	Morton et al. 1967

of pregnancy before twinning can be diagnosed. Furthermore, the data of Nylander (1969) are based on all births.

We must finally consider the Mongoloid peoples of Asia. The available data are set out in Table 4.6. They are mostly based on reasonably large numbers, but as we saw in discussing the Japanese figures earlier they are subject to considerable bias, the rates based on hospital figures tending to be too high and those based on birth registration, particularly before the war, tending to be too low. When allowance has been made for this bias it seems likely that the monozygotic rate is about four per thousand in all cases, but that the dizygotic rate is very low, probably about two and a half per thousand in many Asiatic peoples, although it may be rather higher in some. The data are not reliable enough to justify further analysis of possible differences between different ethnic groups within the Mongoloid race.

In summary, then, the monozygotic twinning rate is constant but the dizygotic twinning rate shows large racial variations. The three main racial groups of mankind have their characteristic dizygotic twinning rates, low in the Mongoloid, high in the Negroid, and intermediate in the Caucasoid. There are also smaller variations within these races, some of which at least seem to be of racial origin. It will be shown in Chapter 6 that the dizygotic but not the monozygotic twinning rate is genetically determined, and it therefore seems likely that these racial differences are of genetic origin. Little is known of the evolutionary factors which through natural selection have led to these differences, but we shall return to this subject in Chapter 8. It is, however, interesting to observe that there is a general rule among mammals that within a species, the race (or breed) which is larger in bodily size will have the larger litter size. This rule is obeyed in man since negroes are in general tall and Mongoloids short with Caucasoids in between.

Nutrition

Undernutrition causes a decrease in the litter size in many mammals. It is well known that sheep fed on a low-plane diet have fewer twins than sheep fed on a high-plane diet (Hammond 1961), and the practice of flushing sheep, that is to say feeding them up before mating in order to increase the number of lambs, is widespread. In wild animals the litter size is larger in years when food is plentiful than when it is scarce; this has been found in arctic foxes, lions, elks, deer, and prairie deermice (Lack 1954).

There is little information about the effect of undernutrition on the twinning rate in man since reliable vital statistics are usually not available during periods of starvation, but data have been published on the twinning rate in several countries during the Second World War (Bulmer 1958b). The mono- zygotic and dizygotic twinning rates before, during, and after the war in France, Holland, Norway, and Sweden are given in Table 4.7 together with the total twinning rate in Denmark

Table 4.7. The twinning rate during the Second World War, stan- dardized for maternal age (Bulmer 1958b)

Country	Period	Monozygotic	Dizygotic
France	1934–40	3·5	7·1
	1941–45	3·7	6·4
	1946–50	3·7	7·1
Holland	1936–40	3·6	7·9
	1941–45	3·9	6·8
	1946–50	3·7	7·7
Norway	1936–40	3·8	8·8
	1941–45	3·9	7·1
	1946–50	4·0	8·2
Sweden	1936–40	3·4	9·6
	1941–45	3·7	8·7
	1946–50	3·2	8·7
Denmark	1936–40	14·8	
	1941–45	14·7	
	1946–50	14·1	

where no sex breakdown is available; the rates have been standardized for maternal age. There is little or no change in the monozygotic rate in any country, but there is a definite fall in the dizygotic rate during the war compared with both the pre-war and the post-war periods in France, Holland, and Norway which suffered considerable undernourishment under German occupation. In neutral Sweden there was a fall in the dizygotic rate during the war but it was not followed by a rise afterwards and is probably attributable to some other cause.

In Denmark, which was leniently treated by the Germans during its occupation and suffered little undernutrition, there is no evidence of a fall in the twinning rate. It is also of interest that the fall in the twinning rate in France does not seem to have affected Brittany and Normandy, which are believed to

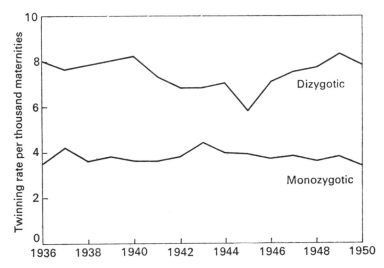

FIG. 4.9. The twinning rate in Holland during the Second World War, standardized for maternal age. (Bulmer 1959b.)

have suffered little during the war because they are such highly agricultural areas (Bulmer 1959b).

There is thus considerable evidence that the dizygotic twinning rate fell during the Second World War in those countries which suffered from undernutrition. This conclusion is strengthened by consideration of the yearly twinning rates in Holland shown in Fig. 4.9. The dizygotic twinning rate was depressed from about eight to about seven per thousand during the whole war, but there was also a sharp fall to below six per thousand in 1945 which corresponds to conceptions during the 'famine winter' of 1944–45 when there was severe starvation in western Holland due to severance of communications after the Allied invasion.

It has also been claimed by Hytten and Leitch (1964) that there was a fall in the dizygotic twinning rate in Hiroshima and Nagasaki in the period after the dropping of the atomic bomb. However, the evidence is rather inconclusive since reference to the paper by Morton (1955) from which the figures were taken shows that stillbirths and neonatal deaths have been excluded; this fact almost certainly explains at least part of the reduction in the twinning rate.

There is thus considerable evidence that undernutrition causes a decrease in the litter size in mammals and a decrease in the dizygotic twinning rate in man. This decrease is probably a consequence of diminished secretion of gonadotrophin by the pituitary, which is known to follow prolonged underfeeding in experimental animals (Burrows 1949, Keys, Brožek, Henschel, Mickelsen, and Taylor 1950). It is possible, however, that part of the decrease in litter size in mammals is due to increased foetal mortality, but this explanation cannot apply to man since there is no decrease in the monozygotic twinning rate. Another possible explanation which cannot be ruled out is a decrease in male fertility.

5 Higher Multiple Births

THERE is no theoretical limit to the number of children that may be born at one time, but reliable reports of births higher than five are extremely rare, if pregnancies following gonado-trophin treatment for infertility are excluded. Even quintuplets are very rare, although they undoubtedly occur from time to time; the most famous example are the Dionne quintuplets, who were probably monozygotic (MacArthur 1938). In this chapter, however, we shall confine our attention to triplets and quadruplets about whom there is enough information to justify a statistical study of their frequency of occurrence.

In 1895 Hellin formulated the law that if the frequency of twins is 1 in 89, then the frequency of triplets will be about 1 in 89^2, the frequency of quadruplets 1 in 89^3, and so on. This empirical law had in fact been established for triplets and quadruplets by several students of national birth statistics before Hellin, and received ample confirmation later (Jenkins 1937, Gedda 1951). However, Hellin's law takes no account of the different types of triplets and quadruplets which may occur or of variation with maternal age. Several attempts have been made to remedy these defects (Jenkins 1927, Jenkins and Gwin 1940, Allen and Firschein 1957, Bulmer 1958a, Allen 1960a). The most satisfactory method seems to be that of Allen (1960a) which represents an extension of Weinberg's differential method supplemented by some plausible assumptions. We shall now apply this method to try to determine the frequencies of the different possible types of triplets and quadruplets, and we shall then discuss what model can be constructed to explain the results.

The frequency of triplets

There are three types of triplets, monozygotic triplets derived from a single ovum which divides twice, dizygotic triplets derived from the release of two ova, one of which then divides, and trizygotic triplets derived from the release of three ova. All the monozygotic triplets must be of the same sex, half the dizygotic triplets will be of the same sex and half of unlike sex (either two boys and one girl or one boy and two girls), while one quarter of the trizygotic triplets will be of the same sex and three quarters of unlike sex. This is shown diagrammatically in Table 5.1.

Table 5.1. The three types of triplets

Type	Monozygotic	Dizygotic	Trizygotic
Origin	0 / \ 0 0 / \ 0 0	0 / \ 0 0	0 0 0
Like-sexed	1	$\frac{1}{2}$	$\frac{1}{4}$
Unliked-sexed	0	$\frac{1}{2}$	$\frac{3}{4}$

Unfortunately there are three types of triplets and only two sex types, so that Weinberg's method of estimating monozygotic and dizygotic twins cannot be extended to triplets unless some further assumption is made. It seems reasonable to suppose, however, that if m and d are the monozygotic and dizygotic twinning rates, then the frequency of dizygotic triplets will be $2md$; for the probability that two ova will be released is d and the probability that one or other of them will divide to produce dizygotic triplets is $2m$. If the total number of births is N, then the number of dizygotic triplets will be $2Nmd$. When age-specific twinning rates are available it is best to estimate the numbers of dizygotic triplets separately for each maternal age group and then to add them up in order to allow for the variation of the twinning rate with maternal age, but the effect of ignoring this refinement is probably small.

Having estimated the number of dizygotic triplets as T_2, say, we now argue that half of them will be like-sexed and half unlike-sexed. Hence, if U is the number of unlike-sexed triplets, then $(U - \frac{1}{2}T_2)$ will be the number of unlike-sexed triplets who are not dizygotic; but this is three quarters of the trizygotic triplets, so that the total number of trizygotic triplets can be estimated as

$$T_3 = \tfrac{4}{3} (U - \tfrac{1}{2}T_2).$$

The number of monozygotic triplets can now be estimated by the remainder, that is to say by

$$T_1 = L + U - T_2 - T_3 = L - \tfrac{1}{3}U - \tfrac{1}{3}T_2$$

where L is the number of like-sexed triplets. The sampling variances of these estimates can be found approximately by assuming that L and U are independent Poisson variates and that T_2 is known exactly (cf. p. 72).

This method of estimation was suggested by Allen in 1960. Its validity depends on the correctness of the assumption that the frequency of dizygotic triplets is $2md$. This assumption would be very plausible if we could measure the frequencies of twins and triplets shortly after conception before any of them had died, but unfortunately we can only measure their frequencies at birth, and there is no way of telling how many twins were once triplets or how many singletons were once twins or even triplets. If there is appreciable pre-natal mortality the assumption on which the method rests may thus be invalid. However, the internal consistency of the results obtained by this method lead me to believe that it is essentially correct.

Data on the numbers of triplets by sex-type have been published by four countries, England and Wales, U.S.A., Italy, and Japan; the data are shown in Table 5.2 together with estimates of the frequencies of the three types of triplets obtained by the above method. It is particularly interesting to compare the Japanese figures with the others in view of the low frequency of dizygotic twins in that country. The frequency of monozygotic triplets is fairly constant at about twenty per million in all four countries; this would be expected since the

Table 5.2. The numbers of triplets in different countries and the estimated frequencies of the three types of triplet

	England and Wales 1938–62	U.S.A. 1922–54	Italy 1933–54	Japan 1956
Like-sexed triplets	931	4090	1494	73
Unlike-sexed triplets	999	3741	1596	28
Dizygotic triplets (estimated)	1092	4138	1556	34
Total maternities (millions)	17·70	71·05	20·82	1·82
Monozygotic triplet frequency (per million)	13	21	21	28
Dizygotic triplet frequency (per million)	62	58	75	19
Trizygotic triplet frequency (per million)	34	31	52	8

monozygotic twinning rate shows little racial variation. The frequency of dizygotic triplets is again fairly constant at about sixty per million in the three Caucasian countries, but falls sharply to about twenty per million in Japan; this is a direct consequence of the low dizygotic twinning rate there, since the frequency of dizygotic triplets has been calculated from the frequencies of monozygotic and dizygotic twins. The most interesting result is the frequency of trizygotic triplets, which is fairly constant at about forty per million in the three Caucasian countries, but drops to ten per million in Japan; this result would also be expected in view of the low dizygotic twinning rate there. The rather high frequencies of dizygotic and trizygotic triplets in Italy compared with England and Wales and U.S.A. is probably a result of the higher average maternal age, since the figures are not corrected for this factor. The rather low frequency of monozygotic triplets in England and Wales is unexplained, but may be a sampling error.

Hellin's law suggests that the frequencies of monozygotic

Table 5.3. Estimated frequencies of monozygotic and trizygotic triplets by maternal age and their relationship to the squares of the frequencies of monozygotic and dizygotic twins (England and Wales, 1938–62)

Mother's age	Under 25	25–30	30–35	35–40	Over 40
Monozygotic triplet frequency (per million)	13	12	11	19	18
Trizygotic triplet frequency (per million)	12	24	58	78	41
Monozygotic triplet frequency/m^2	1·1	1·0	0·8	1·3	1·3
Trizygotic triplet frequency/d^2	0·46	0·32	0·44	0·43	0·51

and trizygotic triplets might respectively be proportional to the squares of the frequencies of monozygotic and dizygotic twins. It is therefore interesting to consider how the frequencies of these two types of triplets vary with maternal age. Data on the numbers of triplets broken down simultaneously by sex and maternal age are available for England and Wales and have been used to calculate the frequencies of monozygotic and trizygotic triplets by maternal age; the results are shown in Table 5.3. The frequency of monozygotic triplets does not vary appreciably with maternal age, as might be expected since there is only a slight rise in the monozygotic twinning rate with age. On the other hand, the frequency of trizygotic triplets varies greatly with age and resembles the dizygotic twinning rate in its behaviour, rising to a maximum at age thirty-five to forty and then decreasing. Futhermore, the ratio of the monozygotic triplet frequency to the square of the monozygotic twinning rate is nearly equal to 1 at all ages, while the corresponding ratio of the trizygotic triplet frequency to the square of the dizygotic twinning rate is also constant and is about 0·4 at all ages.

It can therefore be concluded that

$$\text{monozygotic triplet frequency} = k_1 m^2$$

$$\text{trizygotic triplet frequency} = k_3 d^2$$

The possible reasons for this relationship will be considered later. The constants, k_1 and k_3, can be estimated more precisely from the combined data for England and Wales, U.S.A., and Italy by the formulae

$$k_1 = \frac{\text{Total monozygotic triplets}}{\Sigma N m^2}$$

$$k_3 = \frac{\text{Total trizygotic triplets}}{\Sigma N d^2}$$

where m and d are the age-specific monozygotic and dizygotic twinning rates in each country, N is the number of maternities in the same age group and country, and the summation sign indicates summation over age and country. The combined estimates obtained in this way, with their standard errors, are

$$k_1 = 1\cdot36 \pm 0\cdot04$$

$$k_3 = 0\cdot47 \pm 0\cdot01$$

A breakdown of the frequency of triplets by maternal age but not by sex is also available for U.S.A. and France. Table 5.4 shows the frequency of triplets by maternal age in these two countries as observed and as predicted by the formula

$$\text{Frequency of triplets} = 1\cdot36 m^2 + 2md + 0\cdot47 d^2$$

It will be seen that the agreement between the observed and the predicted frequencies is very good for France and moderately good for U.S.A. This provides further confirmation of the model that the frequencies of monozygotic, dizygotic, and trizygotic triplets are $1.36m^2$, $2md$, and $0.47d^2$ respectively. We shall now consider briefly the foetal membranes of triplets about which a limited amount of information is available. It will be remembered from Chapter 2 that dizygotic

Table 5.4. The frequency of triplets per million maternities by maternal age

Mother's age	Under 20	20–25	25–30	30–35	35–40	Over 40
U.S.A., 1923–36 and 1949–54						
Observed	37	61	103	157	222	147
Predicted	34	65	105	166	234	164
France, 1920–49						
Observed		49	87	135	182	125
Predicted		51	81	137	178	136

twins are all dichorial, and that one-third of monozygotic twins are dichorial and two-thirds monochorial. We should therefore expect that all trizygotic triplets will be trichorial, and that one-third of dizygotic triplets will be trichorial and two-thirds dichorial. If we assume that the times of division of the embryo to form monozygotic triplets are independent (although this may not be true in practice), we should expect one-ninth of monozygotic triplets to be trichorial, four-ninths dichorial, and four-ninths monochorial. We shall also assume that mono-, di-, and trizygotic triplets occur in the approximate ratios of 1:2:3 in white populations (see Table 5.2, p. 98) from which it follows that among like-sexed triplets the three types should be in the ratios of 2:3:1, and that half the unlike-sexed triplets should be dizygotic and half trizygotic. We can now calculate the expected frequencies of chorial types in like-sexed and unlike-sexed triplets under the above assumptions. In Table 5.5 the predicted distribution is compared with the observed distribution in thirty-eight reported cases (Saniter 1901, Williams 1926, Steiner

1935, Potter and Fuller 1949). It will be seen that the agreement is quite good ($\chi^2 = 2\cdot8$ with three degrees of freedom).

Confirmation of the above results on the frequencies of the three types of triplets has come from an investigation of the blood groups of fifty-four sets of like-sexed Swedish triplets by Hauge, Herrlin, and Heiken (1967). It was found that seventeen sets were probably monozygotic, twenty-eight dizygotic,

Table 5.5. The distribution of chorial types in triplets

No. of choria		1	2	3	Total
Like-sexed	Observed	4	10	7	21
	Expected	3	10	8	21
Unlike-sexed	Observed	0	9	8	17
	Expected	0	6	11	17

and nine trizygotic, which is in almost perfect agreement with the ratio of $2:3:1$ predicted for like-sexed triplets in white populations.

The frequency of quadruplets

There are four types of quadruplets derived from one, two, three, or four ova. Furthermore, the first two types can each be split into two sub-types, which I call symmetrical and asymmetrical, according to their mode of development. Symmetrical monozygotic quadruplets are formed from monozygotic twins each of which divides again, while asymmetrical monozygotic quadruplets are formed from monozygotic twins one of which divides twice again. Similarly, symmetrical dizygotic quadruplets are formed from dizygotic twins each of which divides, whereas asymmetrical dizygotic quadruplets are formed from dizygotic twins one of which divides twice into monozygotic triplets. These types are set out diagrammatically in Table 5.6 together with the distribution within them of the three possible sex types (all of the same sex, three of the same sex and one of different sex, or two of each sex). It should be

Table 5.6. The types of quadruplets

Type	Symmetrical monozygotic	Asymmetrical monozygotic	Symmetrical dizygotic	Asymmetrical dizygotic	Trizygotic	Tetrazygotic
Origin						
Frequency 4:0	1	1	$\frac{1}{2}$	$\frac{1}{2}$	$\frac{1}{4}$	$\frac{1}{8}$
of 3:1	0	0	0	$\frac{1}{2}$	$\frac{1}{2}$	$\frac{1}{2}$
sex types 2:2	0	0	$\frac{1}{2}$	0	$\frac{1}{4}$	$\frac{3}{8}$

noted that symmetrical and asymmetrical dizygotic quadruplets differ in the distribution of sex types within them. The numbers of quadruplets by sex type are available for England and Wales, U.S.A., France, and Italy. The combined data from these four countries are shown in Table 5.7 together

Table 5.7. Numbers of quadruplets by type. See text for explanation

Sex type	4:0	3:1	2:2	Total	Frequency per million maternities
Monozygotic	37	0	0	37	0·29
Symmetrical dizygotic	7	0	7	14	0·11
Asymmetrical dizygotic	20	20	0	40	0·32
Trizygotic	13	26	13	52	0·42
Tetrazygotic	9	31	30	70	0·56
Total	86	77	50	213	1·70

with estimates of the numbers of the different types of quadruplets which have been obtained in the following way. The number of symmetrical dizygotic quadruplets has been estimated on the assumption that the probability of this type is m^2d, since they are derived from the release of two ova (probability d) each of which divides into monozygotic twins (probability m^2, on the assumption that the two divisions are independent); after estimating this number at each maternal age in each country I have divided the total number of fourteen equally between sex types 4:0 and 2:2. Similarly the number of asymmetrical dizygotic quadruplets has been estimated on the assumption that the probability of this type is $2 \cdot 72m^2d$ since they are derived from the release of two ova (probability d) one each of which divides into monozygotic triplets (probability $2 \times 1 \cdot 36m^2$ since there are two ova which can do this); the total estimated number of forty has been divided equally between sex types 4:0 and 3:1. Finally, the number of trizygotic quadruplets has been estimated on the assumption that the probability of this type is $1 \cdot 41d^2$ since the probability that three ova will be released is $0.47d^2$ and the probability that one of them will divide is $3m$; the total number of fifty-two quadruplets calculated from this formula has been divided among the three sex types in the ratio of $1:2:1$.

There now remain forty-six quadruplets of sex type $4:0$, thirty-one of type $3:1$ and thirty of type $2:2$ to be allocated as monozygotic or tetrazygotic quadruplets. All the sixty-one quadruplets which are not like-sexed must be tetrazygotic and should furthermore form seven-eighths of these quadruplets. We may therefore estimate the total number of tetrazygotic quadruplets as seventy and the number of monozygotic quadruplets as thirty-seven; no distinction can be made between symmetrical and asymmetrical monozygotic quadruplets.†

A check on the validity of these calculations can be obtained by comparing the proportions of tetrazygotic quadruplets of sex types $3:1$ and $2:2$; the observed proportion of $31:30$ is not far from the expected proportion of $4:3$. It would however be too much to hope that these calculations give more than a very approximate idea of the frequencies of the different types of quadruplets. It is nevertheless worth considering how the frequencies of monozygotic and tetrazygotic quadruplets might be related to the frequencies of the corresponding types of twins. If it can be assumed that the frequency of monozygotic quadruplets is proportional to m^3, then the constant of proportionality can be estimated by dividing the number of monozygotic quadruplets by ΣNm^3 (cf. p. 100); in this way the frequency of monozygotic quadruplets is found to be $5.4m^3$. Similarly, the frequency of tetrazygotic quadruplets is found to be about $0.72d^3$ on the assumption that this frequency is proportional to d^3.

† Since one degree of freedom remains it might seem preferable not to use the calculated number of symmetrical dizygotic quadruplets which is based on the slightly dubious assumption that the two divisions are independent. However, it is likely that the increase in the sampling error introduced by estimating this frequency would be greater than the possible bias introduced by the assumption of independence.

On the above model the total frequency of quadruplets at each maternal age should be

$$5 \cdot 4m^3 + 3 \cdot 7m^2d + 1 \cdot 4md^2 + 0 \cdot 72d^3$$

since the terms in this sum are respectively the frequencies of monozygotic, dizygotic, trizygotic, and tetrazygotic quadruplets. Data on the frequency of quadruplets by age are available

Table 5.8. The frequency of quadruplets per million maternities by maternal age

Maternal age	Under 25	25–30	30–35	Over 35
Observed frequency	0·6	1·3	2·3	3·7
Predicted frequency	0·6	1·3	2·4	3·4

for England and Wales, U.S.A., and France. The combined data are presented in Table 5.8 and show good agreement with the predicted frequencies.

The above results are confirmed by the limited number of

Table 5.9. Numbers of quadruplets of known zygosity

Type	Observed	Predicted
Monozygotic	3	5
Symmetrical dizygotic	2	2
Asymmetrical dizygotic	5	5
Trizygotic	8	7
Tetrazygotic	10	9
Total	28	28

quadruplets in the literature whose probable zygosity diagnosis is known. This subject has been reviewed independently by Hamilton, Brown, and Spiers (1959) and by Allen (1960b), who altogether consider twenty-eight case reports. The combined data are summarized in Table 5.9 and show good agreement with the numbers predicted from Table 5.7.

A theoretical model of multiple births

We have found that the frequencies of monozygotic triplets and quadruplets are about $1\cdot36m^2$ and $5\cdot4m^3$ respectively, and that the frequencies of trizygotic triplets and of tetrazygotic quadruplets are about $0\cdot47d^2$ and $0\cdot72d^3$ respectively, where m and d are the frequencies of monozygotic and dizygotic twins. These estimates depend on the validity of the assumptions made in calculating the frequencies of dizygotic triplets and of dizygotic and trizygotic quadruplets, but confidence in them is confirmed by their correct prediction of the variation of the frequencies of triplets and quadruplets with maternal age and by their agreement with the limited data available on the chorial types of triplets and on the numbers of triplets and quadruplets whose zygosity is known directly. It is therefore interesting to compare these results with the simplest statistical model which can be constructed to account for them.

We consider first the process of multiple ovulation which leads to the production of dizygotic twins, trizygotic triplets, and tetrazygotic quadruplets. The simplest model is that the production of extra ova is a completely random process and that the number of extra ova released follows a Poisson distribution. It follows that the probability that r extra ova will be released, so that there are $r + 1$ ova altogether, is approximately $d^r/r!$. (This result is derived in the Appendix to this chapter.) On this model the frequencies of trizygotic triplets and of tetrazygotic quadruplets should be equal to $\frac{1}{2}d^2$ and $\frac{1}{6}d^3$ respectively.

The estimated frequencies of trizygotic and of tetrazygotic quadruplets are $0\cdot47d^2$ and $0\cdot72d^3$ respectively. It would therefore appear at first sight that the frequency of trizygotic triplets is in good agreement with the Poisson model, but that the frequency of tetrazygotic quadruplets is increased. However, we have so far ignored the important fact, which will be discussed in the next chapter, that the probability of having dizygotic twins varies greatly from mother to mother. If we write p for the probability of dizygotic twinning in a particular mother, and $d = E(p)$ for the average value of p in the population of mothers, then it will be shown in the next chapter that

$$E(p^2) = 4d^2$$

$$E(p^3) = 36d^3.$$

Hence, if the frequencies of trizygotic triplets and tetrazygotic quadruplets are $\frac{1}{2}p^2$ and $\frac{1}{6}p^3$ respectively for a particular mother, then the frequencies of these types of multiple birth in the population should be

$$E(\tfrac{1}{2}p^2) = 2d^2$$

and

$$E(\tfrac{1}{6}p^3) = 6d^3$$

respectively. These theoretical values are much higher than the estimated frequencies. It can be concluded that the release of extra ova is not a completely random process but that some process of control reduces the number of higher multiple ovulations below the number which might be expected from the number of double ovulations. Little is known about the physiology of the mechanism which controls the number of ova released and which ensures that in man only one ovum is usually released, but in view of its probable complexity it is perhaps not surprising that it cannot be regarded as a completely random phenomenon.

We turn now to the division of the ovum into two, three, or more embryos to produce monozygotic twins, triplets, quadruplets, and so on. The simplest model for such a process is the pure birth process, which is sometimes known as the Yule process since it was first used by Yule (1924) in connection with the number of species in a genus, and which has been used subsequently as a model for bacterial growth, and in cascade theory in physics. In this model it is supposed that each 'particle' (for example, a species, a bacterium, a physical particle, or in the present context an embryo) has a small, independent chance of splitting into two in a short time interval.

It is shown in the Appendix to this chapter that under these assumptions the frequency of monozygotic triplets should be m^2, the frequency of monozygotic quadruplets m^3, and so on. The frequency of monozygotic triplets has in fact been estimated as $1 \cdot 36 m^2$, which is in quite good agreement with the theoretical value, but the estimated frequency of monozygotic quadruplets is $5 \cdot 4 m^3$, more than five times its theoretical frequency. One possible explanation of this increase is that the chance of having monozygotic twins varies from mother to mother in the same way as the chance of dizygotic twinning though to a far smaller extent. It will be seen in the next chapter that there is no positive evidence of such variability in the monozygotic twinning rate, but it would be difficult to detect in the presence of the very high variability of dizygotic twinning and the possibility must remain open. Several other explanations might be put forward to account for the increase in the frequency of monozygotic quadruplets, but it does not seem profitable to discuss them in the absence of further evidence. It is perhaps more surprising that such a simple model should hold approximately for monozygotic triplets than that it should break down for quadruplets.

Appendix: The Poisson and Yule Processes

The Poisson process

Suppose that events occur at random in time at an average rate of λ per unit time. In a short interval of time, dt, there is a chance λdt that an event will occur and a chance $1-\lambda dt$ that no event will occur, if dt is small enough to make the chance that more than one event will occur negligible. If $P_r(t)$ is the probability that exactly r events have occurred by time t, then the probability that r events have occurred by time $t+dt$ is

$$P_r(t+dt) = P_r(t)(1-\lambda dt)+P_{r-1}(t)\lambda dt$$

since this can happen in two ways: (1) r events occur by time t, and no events between times t and $t+dt$; (2) $r-1$ events occur by time t, and one event between t and $t+dt$. (To make this equation true for $r = 0$ we must put $P_{-1}(t) = 0$, since only the first possibility exists in this case.) If we rearrange this equation and then let dt tend to zero we obtain the differential equation.

$$\frac{dP_r(t)}{dt} = \lambda(P_{r-1}(t)-P_r(t))$$

whose solution is

$$P_r(t) = \frac{e^{-\lambda t}(\lambda t)^r}{r!}$$

if we start with no events at time zero. This is the Poisson distribution with mean λt.

To apply this model to multiple ovulations we suppose that extra ova may be released during a fixed time t. Since the average number of extra ova produced, λt, is small we may write approximately

$$P_r = \frac{(\lambda t)^r}{r!} = \frac{P_1^r}{r!} = \frac{d^r}{r!}$$

where $P_1 = d$ is the frequency of dizygotic twins.

The Yule process

Suppose that particles in a population divide at random at an average rate of λ per unit time per particle. The probability that a particular particle will divide into two in the short time interval, dt, is λdt. If there are r particles at time t, there is therefore a probability $r\lambda dt$ that one new particle will have appeared by time $t+dt$, and a probability $1-r\lambda dt$ that no new particle will have appeared. (It is assumed that dt is so small that the chance of more than one particle splitting is negligible.) If $P_r(t)$ is the probability that there are r particles at time t, then the probability that there are r particles at time $t+dt$ is

$$P(t_r+dt) = P_r(t)(1-r\lambda dt)+P_{r-1}(t)(r-1)\lambda dt$$

since this event can only happen in one of two ways: (1) there are r particles at time t and none of them divides in the interval $(t, t+dt)$; (2) there are $r-1$ particles at time t and one of them divides before $t+dt$. If we rearrange this equation and then let dt tend to zero we obtain the differential equation

$$\frac{dP_r(t)}{dt} = \lambda[(r-1)P_{r-1}(t)-rP_r(t)]$$

whose solution is

$$P_r(t) = e^{-\lambda t}(1-e^{-\lambda t})^{r-1}$$

if there is one particle at zero time. When λt is small this equation becomes very nearly

$$P_r(t) = (\lambda t)^{r-1} = P_2{}^{r-1}(t).$$

In these equations λ is the rate of division per particle. In many cases it is not unreasonable to suppose that λ is constant and does not vary with time. In the case of the division of an embryo, however, this is not true since the embryo is more likely to divide at some periods of its life history than at others; we must therefore allow λ to be a function of time, $\lambda(t)$. It can easily be verified that the solution remains the same except that $\int_0^t \lambda(t)dt$ must be substituted for λt. If t is greater than about fourteen days when division of the embryo ceases (i.e. when $\lambda(t)$ becomes zero), $P_2(t)$ is the frequency of monozygotic twins, m. On this model, therefore, the frequency of monozygotic triplets should be m^2, the frequency of monozygotic quadruplets m^3, and so on.

6 The Inheritance of Twinning

THE variability of the dizygotic twinning rate in different races and the constancy of the monozygotic twinning rate suggest that dizygotic, but not monozygotic, twinning is under hereditary control. It is generally believed today that this is so and that the mode of inheritance is confined to the mother. It was suggested by several earlier investigators that the father might also play a role in the inheritance of twinning, but it now seems likely that these results were due to bias in the collection of the data; a few reports that monozygotic twinning might also be inherited can probably be attributed to the same cause. Before we turn to the direct evidence about the inheritance of twinning, however, we shall first consider the repeat frequency of twinning in the same mother which provides valuable information about the amount of variability of twin proneness in the population, although by itself it can provide no information about whether this variability is hereditary or environmental.

The repeat frequency of twinning

The repeat frequency of twinning is the frequency of twinning among women who have already had one set of twins. If all women have the same chance of producing twins then the repeat frequency will be the same as the twinning rate in the general population; if, on the other hand, some women are more likely to have twins than others, whether for genetic or non-genetic reasons, then women who have produced one set of twins will be women who are more prone to produce twins and so the repeat frequency will be higher than the general twinning rate. The repeat frequency can thus be used to estimate the variability of twin proneness in the population, regardless of the cause of this variability.

The first, and the most extensive, data on this subject were obtained by Weinberg from family registers in Stuttgart at the beginning of this century. Weinberg extracted from these registers the reproductive histories of 1 586 women who had borne at least one pair of twins and who had been married at least twenty years. Several other investigations of the repeat frequency have been made, but the only one which reports the sex combinations of the twins in full was made by myself in 1958; the data were obtained from the records of the Manchester Maternity and Child Welfare Department. The analysis of the combined data of Weinberg and myself is presented in Table 6.1.

Table 6.1. The repeat frequency of twinning: combined data of Weinberg (1909) and Bulmer (1958c). See text for explanation.

Propositus	Sibling maternities Unlike-sexed twins	Like-sexed twins	Total	Twinning rate per thousand Monozygotic	Dizygotic
Unlike-sexed twins	58	74	3897	4·1	29·8
Like-sexed twins	74	116	8260	5·1	17·9

To perform this analysis each set of twins was taken in turn as a propositus, and the numbers of like-sexed and unlike-sexed twins among their siblings were counted together with the total number of sibling maternities. These figures were then added up, the data for like-sexed and for unlike-sexed twin propositi being kept separate. The results are shown in the first three columns of Table 6.1. For example, a mother who has had two singletons and one set of like-sexed twins would contribute 2 to the figure 8 260; similarly, a mother with two singletons and two sets of like-sexed twins would contribute 6 to the figure 8 260 and 2 to the figure 116, since each of the twin maternities is taken in turn as a propositus; and a mother with two single-tons, one pair of like-sexed twins, and one pair of unlike-sexed twins would contribute 3 to the figure 3 897, 3 to the figure 8 260, and 1 to each of the figures 74. This is essentially Weinberg's sib method of estimation familiar to human geneticists.

The monozygotic and dizygotic twinning rates among the siblings of like-sexed and unlike-sexed twins can now be calculated by Weinberg's differential method and are shown in the last two columns of Table 6.1. The monozygotic and dizy-gotic twinning rates in the general population may be taken as 3·5 and 7·7 per thousand respectively; these are weighted averages of the rates in Stuttgart and Manchester. There is little or no increase in the monozygotic twinning rate among the siblings of either like-sexed or unlike-sexed twins, but there is a large increase in the dizygotic twinning rate in both groups. Furthermore, the increase in the dizygotic twinning rate among the siblings of unlike-sexed twins ($29·8-7·7=22·1$) is about twice as large as the increase among the siblings of like-sexed twins ($17·9-7·7 = 10·2$); the obvious explanation is that there is no increase among the siblings of monozygotic twins who form half the like-sexed twins. It can therefore be concluded that the increased twinning rate is confined to an increase in the dizygotic twinning rate among the siblings of dizygotic twins; the dizygotic twinning rate in this group is about thirty per thousand which is very nearly four times the dizygotic twinning rate in the general population.

These facts have been confirmed in other studies, notably that of Greulich (1934). Greulich investigated the families of 495 pairs of American twins whose zygosity had in most cases been determined on the basis of similarities or differences in physical characters. Among the siblings of the 273 cases known to be dizygotic there were altogether 299 maternities of whom 26 were twins, giving a total twinning rate of thirty-three per thousand, which is very close to the total twinning rate of thirty-four per thousand among the siblings of unlike-sexed twins in Table 6.1. Among the siblings of the 93 cases known to be monozygotic, on the other hand, there were only 3 pairs of twins in 243 maternities, which represents a rate of twelve per thousand, the same as the rate in the general population.

It must be mentioned that considerably higher repeat frequencies have been found in two investigations. Dahlberg (1952), using Swedish data, found total twinning rates of forty-five per thousand among siblings of unlike-sexed twins and thirty-one per thousand among siblings of like-sexed twins. Similarly, Wyshak and White (1965), using the records of the Mormon Church, have found repeat frequencies of forty-four and twenty-eight per thousand among siblings of unlike-sexed and like-sexed twins respectively. These rates are considerably higher than the corresponding total twinning rates of thirty-four and twenty-three per thousand in Table 6.1. It seems likely that this discrepancy is due to the effect of maternal age. None of the twinning rates in this chapter has been standardized for maternal age since the necessary information is not available except for my own investigation in Manchester. However, it is likely that the distribution of maternal ages among siblings of twins is similar to the distribution among all maternities provided that maternities occurring both before and after each index case are counted; this method was adopted in the analysis of the data of Weinberg (1909), Bulmer (1958c), and Greulich (1934). However, both Dahlberg (1952) and Wyshak and White (1965) considered only maternities subsequent to the index twin maternity and calculated the twinning rate among these subsequent maternities. The average age of these maternities will clearly be higher than that of maternities preceding the index case and will therefore be higher than the average maternal age in the general population; hence the dizygotic twinning rate, which increases rapidly with age, will be spuriously high. It seems likely that this is the explanation of these apparently anomalous results.

There is thus strong evidence that there is a considerable

increase in the repeat frequency and that this increase is confined to its dizygotic component. It can be concluded that the propensity to monozygotic twinning is the same in all women but that the propensity to have dizygotic twins varies from woman to woman. The fact that a woman is known to have had dizygotic twins increases her chances of having dizygotic twins in other pregnancies about fourfold, but if no correction is made for maternal age and if only pregnancies subsequent to the index pregnancy are considered this figure is spuriously increased. The exact significance of this fourfold increase will be considered at the end of this section.

Weinberg (1909) also presented data on the twinning rate among mothers of triplets which are summarized in Table 6.2.

Table 6.2. The twinning rate among mothers of triplets in Württemberg (Weinberg 1909)

Propositus	Sibling maternities		Twinning rate per thousand
	Twins	Total	
Unlike-sexed triplets	81	1355	60
Like-sexed triplets	52	1278	41
All triplets	133	2633	51

It will be seen that the rate is considerably higher than among mothers of twins, and that, as might be expected, it is higher among mothers of unlike-sexed triplets than among mothers of like-sexed triplets. It seems reasonable to assume that the increase in the twinning rate is confined to the dizygotic component, so that the dizygotic twinning rates among the siblings of unlike-sexed, like-sexed, and all triplets are about fifty-six, thirty-seven, and forty-seven per thousand respectively. It also seems reasonable to assume that the twinning rate among siblings of monozygotic triplets (derived from the division into three of a single ovum) is the same as the rate in the general population, while the twinning rate among siblings of dizygotic triplets (derived from the release of two ova, one of which divides into two) is the same as the twinning rate among siblings of dizygotic twins. It remains to estimate the twinning rate among siblings of trizygotic triplets, derived from the simultaneous release of three ova.

It was shown in the last chapter that mono-, di-, and trizygotic triplets occur in the approximate ratios of $1:3:2$. Furthermore if the dizygotic twinning rate in the general population is d, then the dizygotic twinning rates among siblings of monozygotic, dizygotic, and trizygotic triplets will be d, $4d$, and ad respectively, where a is a constant to be estimated representing the increase in the dizygotic twinning rate among siblings of trizygotic triplets. Hence the dizygotic twinning rate among siblings of all triplets will be

$$\tfrac{1}{6}(d \times 1 + 4d \times 3 + ad \times 2) = \tfrac{1}{6}(13 + 2a)d.$$

Putting $d = 0 \cdot 009$, which was the dizygotic twinning rate in Württemberg when the data were collected, and equating the expression to $0 \cdot 047$, the estimated dizygotic twinning rate among siblings of all triplets, we find that $a = 9 \cdot 2$. It may therefore be concluded that the dizygotic twinning rate among mothers of trizygotic triplets is about nine times the rate in the general population, and more than double the rate among mothers of dizygotic twins.

As a check on the validity of this method we can calculate the predicted frequency of twins among mothers of like-sexed and unlike-sexed triplets. It was shown in the last chapter that among like-sexed triplets the three zygotic types of triplets will be in the ratios $2:3:1$, while the unlike-sexed triplets will be dizygotic and trizygotic with equal probability. Assuming the dizygotic twinning rates among siblings of monozygotic, dizygotic, and trizygotic triplets to be nine, thirty-six, and eighty-one per thousand respectively, we find that the dizygotic twinning rates among siblings of like-sexed and unlike-sexed triplets should be about thirty-four and fifty-eight per thousand respectively. These are close to the observed rates of thirty-seven and fifty-six per thousand.

Finally, Weinberg investigated the histories of twenty-two mothers of quadruplets in Württemberg between 1790 and 1900; his data are reproduced in Table 6.3. It will be seen that the

Table 6.3. The twinning rate among mothers of quadruplets in Württemberg, 1790–1900 (Weinberg 1909)

Sex distribution of quadruplets	Sibling maternities Twins	Total	Twinning rate per thousand
4:0	3	70	43
3:1	7	45	156
2:2	4	54	74
Total	14	169	83

twinning rates among these mothers are even greater than among mothers of triplets. By applying the arguments used in the previous three paragraphs to these data we can estimate that the dizygotic twinning rate among siblings of tetrazygotic quadruplets is about fifteen per cent, which is about sixteen times the frequency in the general population. The numbers are clearly too small, however, and the assumptions made too numerous to justify us in placing much reliance on this estimate.

We must now consider how these results can be used to provide a numerical estimate of the variability in the propensity of different women to have dizygotic twins. It will be assumed that if one woman is twice as likely to have dizygotic twins as another when they are both twenty, then the same will be true when they are both thirty, although of course the absolute probabilities will be greater. Under these circumstances a woman's propensity to dizygotic twinning can be measured by her average probability of having such twins, the average being a weighted average over the age distribution of maternities in the population. This probability, which will be denoted by p, is a quantity which varies from one woman to another and can therefore be regarded as a random variable with a probability density function, $f(p)$, and in particular with a mean and

9

a variance. Unfortunately, p cannot be measured directly in a particular woman since several thousand maternities are necessary to measure a twinning rate accurately and so the properties of this distribution must be estimated indirectly. It is clear that the mean of the distribution is the average dizygotic twinning rate in the whole population

$$E(p) = \int_0^1 pf(p)\, dp = d.$$

We shall now show how the variance of the distribution can be estimated from the repeat frequency of twinning among mothers of dizygotic twins.

In the calculation of the dizygotic twinning rate among the siblings of dizygotic twins each mother was counted as often as she had had such twins. This method of calculation ensures that the chance that a mother will be counted is proportional to her chance of having dizygotic twins, and so the distribution of p in this selected group of mothers is, by Bayes' theorem,

$$\frac{pf(p)}{\int_0^1 pf(p)\, dp} = \frac{pf(p)}{d}.$$

The average dizygotic twinning rate among these mothers is the mean value of this distribution, which is

$$\frac{\int_0^1 p^2 f(p)\, dp}{d} = \frac{E(p^2)}{d}.$$

We have found empirically that this frequency is about $4d$, from which we can conclude that

$$E(p^2)/d^2 = 4.$$

Now

$$E(p^2) = V(p) + d^2$$

where $V(p)$ is the variance of the distribution, and so

$$V(p)/d^2 = 3.$$

Put in another way this means that the coefficient of variation of the distribution is $100\sqrt{3} = 170$ per cent, which indicates a high degree of variability. The standard deviation is $d\sqrt{3}$ which is equal to 0·014 if we give d its typical European value of 0·008.

Let us now consider the significance of the fact that the dizygotic twinning rate among mothers of trizygotic triplets is about nine times the rate in the general population. It was shown in the last chapter that there is good reason to suppose that if p is the chance that a woman will have dizygotic twins, then the chance that she will have trizygotic triplets is proportional to p^2. If this is so then it can be shown, by arguments similar to those of the preceding paragraph, that the average chance of having dizygotic twins among mothers of trizygotic triplets is

$$E(p^3)/E(p^2) = E(p^3)/4d^2.$$

Equating this probability to $9d$ we find that

$$E(p^3) = 36d^3.$$

Hence it can be calculated that the skewness of the distribution, measured as the ratio of the third moment about the mean to the cube of the standard deviation, is about $+$ 5. This high degree of skewness indicates that the distribution has a long tail to the right; in other words, there are a few mothers with a high chance of having dizygotic twins. This is indeed obvious from the fact that the estimated frequency of dizygotic twins among mothers of trizygotic triplets in Württemberg is as high as eight per cent; this figure rises to fifteen per cent, if we can believe the calculation, among mothers of tetrazygotic quadruplets.

The familial incidence of twinning

Study of the repeat frequency of twinning has shown that the propensity to have dizygotic twins varies considerably from one mother to another. To find out whether this variability is of genetic or environmental origin we must consider the twinning rate among relatives of parents of twins.

The most extensive, and probably the most reliable, data

on the familial incidence of twinning were obtained by Weinberg (1901, 1909) from family registers in Stuttgart and Württemburg at the beginning of this century; they are summarized in Table 6.4. Weinberg concluded firstly that the inheritance of

Table 6.4. The twinning rate among first-degree relatives of twins and triplets (Weinberg 1901, 1909)

	Twins	Maternities	Twinning rate	Twinning rate in population
Female relatives of mothers of twins and triplets	537	28 318	19·0	12·1
Female relatives of fathers of twins and triplets	95	8 896	10·7	11·2
Female relatives of mothers of unlike-sexed twins	174	7 892	22·0	11·9
Female relatives of mothers of like-sexed twins	255	15 201	16·8	11·9
Female relatives of mothers of monozygotic twins (estimated as difference between like-sexed and unlike-sexed twins)	81	7 309	11·1	11·9

twinning is confined to the female line, since he found an increased twinning rate among the relatives of the mothers of twins but not among the relatives of the fathers (see the first two lines of Table 6.4). He concluded secondly, by comparing the twinning rates among relatives of mothers of like-sexed and of unlike-sexed twins, that the inheritance of twinning is confined to its dizygotic component (see the last three lines of Table 6.4).

It is not surprising to find that monozygotic twinning is not inherited, since we have already seen that there are no racial differences in the monozygotic twinning rate and that there is no increase in the repeat frequency of monozygotic twinning.

It is also quite easy to understand why the inheritance of dizygotic twinning should be limited to the female line if we suppose that the genes responsible act by increasing the frequency of double ovulation, perhaps through increasing the level of pituitary gonadotrophin. On this hypothesis, the genes for dizygotic twinning are carried and transmitted by both men and women in the normal way, but can only express themselves in women because they act through the ovaries. Such genes, which are carried on the autosomal chromosomes in the usual way but whose expression is confined to one sex, are called *sex-limited*. Another example of a sex-limited character is premature baldness, which is thought to be caused by a dominant gene which only expresses itself in men, perhaps because it requires an adequate level of male sex hormone before it can produce baldness.

Weinberg's conclusions have been confirmed in several recent investigations, in particular by Wyshak and White (1965), who used the extensive family records of the Mormon Church, and by Waterhouse (1950), who obtained a sample of twins by public appeal, although there is evidence of bias through self-selection in the latter sample. However, it has also been suggested, in particular by Greulich (1934), who found a twinning rate of 56/2 471 = twenty-three per thousand among sibs of fathers of twins, that the father may also play a role in the inheritance of twinning. In order to explain this discrepant finding I have suggested previously (Bulmer 1960a) that it may be due to bias caused by under-reporting of single births on the father's side of the family. Greulich obtained his information by interviewing the parents of twins about their families, and it seems quite likely that bias has crept in through incomplete knowledge about the father's side of the family since men are less interested in family affairs than women. Greulich indeed remarked that 'the fathers, as a group, seemed not to know as much about the offspring of their brothers and sisters as the mothers knew about those of their sibs. If such is the case, it is possible that the fathers, more often than the mothers,

failed to recall some non-twin-producers among their sibs.'
Greulich thought the bias unlikely to be serious but produced
no evidence to substantiate this view.

Direct evidence of under-reporting of single births on the
father's side of the family is provided by my own investigation
in which the mothers of twins born in Lancashire in 1956–8
were interviewed by health visitors (Bulmer 1960a); the results
are summarized in Table 6.5. It seems very likely that the high

Table 6.5. The twinning rate among siblings of parents of twins
(Bulmer 1960a)

Relative	Twins	Materni- ties	Twin- ning rate	Adjusted materni- ties	Adjusted twinning rate
Brothers of fathers of twins	28	1676	16·7	2053	13·6
Sisters of fathers of twins	37	1941	19·1	2797	13·2
Brothers of mothers of twins	15	1507	10·0		
Sisters of mothers of twins	41	2053	20·0		

twinning rates among the father's brothers and sisters are due
to under-reporting of single births. It will be observed that the
brothers of both parents have fewer children than the sisters.
This can be explained by the difference in age at marriage of
men and women; for example, the mother's brothers will on
the average be the same age as her sisters but will have been
married three years less and will therefore on average have had
fewer children. Detailed calculations show that this factor
would introduce a difference in the number of children between
brothers and sisters of the order observed. (This argument
depends, of course, on the fact that we are considering women
whose reproductive histories are incomplete.) On this theory,
however, the father's brothers should have had the same number
of children as the mother's sisters, since their average length

of marriage will have been the same. It is therefore suggested that the children of the father's sibs have been under-reported. If we estimate the true number of children of the father's brothers and sisters as 2 053 and 2 797 ($= 2\ 053 \times (2\ 053/1\ 507)$) respectively, and if we also suppose that twin maternities, being more memorable, have been fully reported, the corrected twinning rates among the father's brothers and sisters shown in the last column of Table 6.5 are only slightly above the expected rate of 12·5 per thousand.

It is therefore concluded that a true increase in the twinning rate occurs only among the female relatives of mothers of twins, as expected on the hypothesis that the inheritance of dizygotic twinning is sex-limited. This conclusion is confirmed by the fact that in mixed marriages the dizygotic twinning rate is determined entirely by the race of the mother and is independent of the race of the father, as has been shown by Morton, Chung and Mi (1967) for marriages between Mongoloids and Caucasoids in Hawaii. These authors summarize their conclusions as follows: 'The frequency of monozygotic twinning is almost independent of race. . . . However, the frequency of dizygotic twins is much less for Pacific (= Mongoloid) populations than for Caucasoids and depends only on the race of the mother, independent of the father's race. . . . This supports the conclusion from family studies that evidence purporting to show a paternal effect on dizygotic twinning is invalid.'

We must now consider in more detail the dizygotic twinning rate among female relatives of mothers of dizygotic twins in order to determine more precisely the mode of inheritance. The available data are shown in Table 6.6. (The data of Waterhouse (1950) have been excluded since they seem to be biased through self-selection, but the data of Greulich (1934) and Bulmer (1960a) are included since there is no evidence of bias in their figures on the mother's side of the family.) It will be seen that the dizygotic twinning rate among mothers and daughters of mothers of dizygotic twins is a little less than twice the rate in the general population, while the rate among sisters is increased about two and a half fold.

To interpret these figures genetically we must convert them into correlation coefficients. We shall write p for the probability

Table 6.6. The twinning rate among relatives of mothers of dizygotic twins

Relative	Author	Twins	Materni-ties	Twinning rate	Dizygotic twinning rate†	Dizygotic twinning rate in population	Ratio
Mothers of mothers of unlike-sexed twins in Stuttgart	Weinberg 1909	42	1994	21·1	17·6	7·4	2·4
Mothers of mothers of unlike-sexed twins in Württemburg	Weinberg 1909	42	1864	22·5	19·0	10·7	1·8
Daughters of mothers of unlike-sexed twins in Stuttgart	Weinberg 1909	31	1920	16·2	12·7	7·4	1·7
Daughters of mothers of unlike-sexed twins	Wyshak and White 1965	65	3822	17·0	13·5	(8·0)	(1·6)
Total, Mother or Daughter		180	9600	18·8	15·3	8·3	1·8
Sisters of mothers of unlike-sexed twins in Stuttgart	Weinberg 1909	33	1382	23·9	20·4	7·4	2·8
Sisters of mothers of unlike-sexed twins in Württemburg	Weinberg 1909	26	732	35·5	32·0	10·7	3·0
Sisters of mothers of physically dissimilar twins	Greulich 1934	28	1127‡	24·8	21·3	(8·0)	(2·7)
Sisters of mothers of dizygotic twins§	Bulmer 1960a	32	1369	23·4	19·9	8·9	2·2
Total, Sisters		119	4610	25·8	22·3	8·5	2·6

† Estimated by subtracting 3·5 from figure in previous column
‡ Estimated from internal evidence
§ Estimated from figures for sisters of mothers of all twins by assuming that one-third of the latter are monozygotic and that monozygotic twinning is not inherited

that a woman will have dizygotic twins and p' for the corresponding probability in her relative, and we shall denote the distribution of p in the general population by $f(p)$, the conditional distribution of p' given p by $g(p'|p)$ and the joint distribution of p and p' by $h(p,p')$; it follows from the definition of these quantities that

$$h(p,p') = f(p) \times g(p'|p).$$

It was shown in the last section that the distribution of p among mothers of dizygotic twins, counting each mother as often as she has had such twins, is $pf(p)/d$; hence the probability that such a mother will have twinning rate p and that her relative will have twinning rate p' is

$$\frac{pf(p)}{d} \times g(p'|p) = \frac{ph(p,p')}{d}$$

and so the Expected value of p' among relatives of such mothers is

$$\int_0^1 \int_0^1 \frac{pp'h(p,\,p')}{d}\, dp\, dp' = \frac{E(pp')}{d} = \frac{Covariance + d^2}{d}$$

We also found in the last section that the variance of the distribution was $3d^2$; hence, if we divide the dizygotic twinning rate among relatives of mothers of dizygotic twins by three times the rate in the general population and then subtract $\frac{1}{3}$ we obtain the covariance divided by the variance which is the correlation coefficient. We can therefore conclude that the mother–daughter correlation is about $0{\cdot}8/3 = 0{\cdot}3$ and the sister–sister correlation about $1{\cdot}6/3 = 0{\cdot}5$.

We must now consider the significance of these results. It is shown in the Appendix to this chapter that the total variance of a quantitative character can be split up into a genetic and an environmental component

$$V = V_G + V_E$$

where V is the total variance, V_G the genetic variance, and V_E the environmental variance. The genetic variance can in turn be divided into an additive variance, V_A, and a dominance variance, V_D:

$$V_G = V_A + V_D.$$

If there is no dominance all the genetic variance is additive, but if there is dominance in some or all of the genes controlling the character, then part of the genetic variance will be additive and part dominance. The relative magnitude of the dominance variance depends on the gene frequencies as well as on the degree of dominance. In the case of a completely recessive gene with a population frequency q, the ratio of the additive to the dominance variance is $2q/(1-q)$. When q is small nearly all the genetic variance is dominance variance, but when q is nearly 1, that is to say in the case of a dominant gene with a low frequency, nearly all the genetic variance is additive. When $q = \frac{1}{2}$, two-thirds of the genetic variance is additive and one-third dominance.

The importance of these components of variance is that they determine the correlations between relatives. Under random mating and in the absence of maternal effects it is shown in the Appendix that the mother–daughter covariance is $\frac{1}{2}V_A$ and the sister–sister covariance $\frac{1}{2}V_A + \frac{1}{4}V_D$. The correlation coefficients are obtained by dividing these covariances by the total variance, $V = V_A + V_D + V_E$. If all the variance is additive genetic, then the correlation coefficients attain their maximum value of $\frac{1}{2}$. The presence of environmental variance will decrease both coefficients to the same extent, as might be expected, while the presence of dominance variance will decrease the mother–daughter correlation more than the sister–sister correlation. In the case of a completely recessive gene with population frequency q and in the absence of environmental variance, the correlations are

$$\text{Mother–daughter correlation} = q/(1+q)$$

$$\text{Sister–sister correlation} = [q + \frac{1}{4}(1-q)]/(1+q)$$

When q is small the mother–daughter correlation becomes zero and the sister–sister correlation $\frac{1}{4}$; when q is nearly 1 both correlations become $\frac{1}{2}$ since all the variance is additive; when $q = \frac{1}{2}$ the mother–daughter correlation is 0·33 and the sister–sister correlation 0·42.

We must now try to interpret the estimated correlations of 0·3 for mother–daughter and 0·5 for sister–sister. In view of the rather large sampling errors and of the very indirect method of estimation, and also in view of the known difficulty of using human correlations to partition variation into its components because of the complications of assortative mating and covariance due to common environment, which will be discussed in the next chapter, it would not be justified to press the analysis too closely. It is sufficient to observe that the excess of the sister–sister correlation over the mother–daughter correlation probably indicates a considerable amount of dominance variance, and that the correlations are not very different from those expected from a completely recessive gene with a population frequency of $\frac{1}{2}$; this is of course the same, as far as the correlations between relatives are concerned, as a completely dominant gene with a population frequency of $\frac{1}{2}$.

Let us therefore assume as a working hypothesis that dizygotic twinning is controlled by a pair of genes, T and t, and that women with either of the genotypes TT or Tt have dizygotic twinning rate p_1, while women with the genotype tt have twinning rate p_2. If p_2 is greater than p_1 it means that a high dizygotic twinning rate is determined by the recessive gene t, whereas if p_1 is greater than p_2 dizygotic twinning is determined by the dominant gene T. We shall also suppose, in accordance with the tentative conclusion of the previous paragraph, that these two genes are equally frequent, from which it follows from the Hardy-Weinberg law of population genetics that the frequencies of p_1 and p_2 under random mating are $\frac{3}{4}$ and $\frac{1}{4}$ respectively. Now it was shown in the previous section, from a study of the repeat frequency of twinning, that $E(p^2) = 4d^2$, where d is the mean of the distribution. Hence

$$E(p) = \tfrac{3}{4}p_1 + \tfrac{1}{4}p_2 = d$$

$$E(p^2) = \tfrac{3}{4}p_1^2 + \tfrac{1}{4}p_2^2 = 4d^2$$

The two mathematically possible solutions of these equations are $p_1 = 0$, $p_2 = 4d$ and $p_1 = 2d$, $p_2 = -2d$. Since the twinning rate cannot be negative the only meaningful solution is $p_1 = 0$, $p_2 = 4d$. This solution implies that dizygotic twinning is controlled by a completely recessive gene and that only women with the double recessive genotype *tt* are capable of producing dizygotic twins. These women comprise about one-quarter of the population, among Caucasoids, and have a twinning rate of about thirty-two per thousand, if we give *d* a typical Caucasoid value of about eight per thousand.

Further evidence of the recessive nature of the inheritance of dizygotic twinning is provided by the fact that women of mixed racial origin have a dizygotic twinning rate smaller than would be expected with additive gene action, that is to say, closer to the race with a low dizygotic twinning rate than would be expected from the amount of racial mixture. Thus Morton, Chung, and Mi (1967) found in Hawaii that 'mothers who are hybrids between Caucasoids and Pacific (= Mongoloid) races have a low dizygotic frequency closely resembling that of Pacific mothers'. The same authors discuss the evidence about negro–white crosses provided by comparing pure negroes in Africa with American and Brazilian negroes who have a considerable Caucasoid admixture; they conclude that 'negro-Caucasoid crosses, even in populations that are predominantly negro, lie closer to the Caucasian mean than to the available samples of African negroes'.

Unfortunately this simple genetic model is unable to explain the facts about the frequency of twinning among mothers of triplets and quadruplets which were discussed in the previous section. We estimated there that the dizygotic twinning rate among mothers of trizygotic triplets is about nine times the rate in the general population, and more than double the rate among mothers of dizygotic twins; if, however, there were only one type of mother capable of producing dizygotic twins, as the model suggests, then the dizygotic twinning rate among mothers of trizygotic triplets should be the same as the repeat frequency among mothers of dizygotic twins, since in both cases the mothers are known to be of genotype *tt*. Putting this in another way, we have estimated the skewness of the distribution of p to be about $+5$, which indicates that the distribution has a long tail to the right and that there is a small proportion of mothers with a very high chance of having dizygotic twins, whereas on the model described above the skewness is only $+1\cdot2$. To account for these facts we must therefore postulate the existence of a rather rare third type of mother with a considerably higher propensity to dizygotic twinning, of the order of ten per cent or more, caused either by genetic or by environmental factors. At this point the limits of profitable speculation have probably been reached.

Appendix: *Quantitative Genetics*

Partitioning the variance

If y is the phenotypic value, that is to say the observed value, of some quantitative character, then we may write

$$y = \mu + g + e \tag{6.1}$$

where μ is the mean value in the population, g is the deviation from the mean caused by genetic factors, and e is the deviation caused by environmental factors. If the genetic and environmental deviations are uncorrelated with each other, as they must be if these quantities are suitably defined (Falconer 1960, pp. 132–3), it follows that the total variance can be split into two additive components,

$$V = V_G + V_E \tag{6.2}$$

where

$$V = V(y) = \text{total variance}$$
$$V_G = V(g) = \text{genetic variance} \tag{6.3}$$
$$V_E = V(e) = \text{environmental variance.}$$

We shall now show how the genetic variance in a randomly mating population can be split into two additive components, the additive variance (V_A) and the dominance variance (V_D):

$$V_G = V_A + V_D \tag{6.4}$$

Consider first a single locus with an arbitrary number of alleles in which the frequency of the ith allele is p_i, and let us write g_{ij} for the genetic deviation of an individual who has received the ith allele from his father and the jth allele from his mother. Clearly $g_{ij} = g_{ji}$, and furthermore in a population mating at random the probability of g_{ij} is $p_i p_j$.

We shall now define

$$\alpha_i = \sum_j g_{ij} p_j$$

$$d_{ij} = g_{ij} - \alpha_i - \alpha_j \qquad (6.5)$$

α_i is the average effect of the ith gene, averaged over all genotypes in which it occurs, and d_{ij} is the dominance deviation, that is to say, the difference between the actual value of g_{ij} and the value which would have held if the two genes were additive in their effects. α_i, α_j, and d_{ij} are random variables which have zero Expected values since

$$E(\alpha_i) = \sum_i \alpha_i p_i = \sum_{i,j} g_{ij} p_i p_j = E(g_{ij}) = 0$$

$$E(d_{ij}) = E(g_{ij}) - E(\alpha_i) - E(\alpha_j) = 0 \qquad (6.6)$$

α_i and α_j are clearly independent since they are contributed by different parents. d_{ij} is not independent of α_i, but they are uncorrelated since

$$\mathrm{Cov}(\alpha_i, d_{ij}) = \sum_{i,j} \alpha_i d_{ij} p_i p_j = \sum_i \alpha_i p_i \sum_j d_{ij} p_j \qquad (6.7)$$

which is zero since

$$\sum_j d_{ij} p_j = \sum_j g_{ij} p_j - \alpha_i \sum_j p_j - \sum_j \alpha_j p_j = \alpha_i - \alpha_i = 0 \qquad (6.8)$$

It follows from the identity

$$g_{ij} = \alpha_i + \alpha_j + d_{ij} \qquad \text{(see (6.5))}$$

that

$$V_G = V(\alpha_i) + V(\alpha_j) + V(d_{ij}) \qquad (6.9)$$

If we define

$$V_A = V(\alpha_i) + V(\alpha_j)$$

$$V_D = V(d_{ij}) \tag{6.10}$$

if follows immediately that

$$V_G = V_A + V_D \qquad \text{(see (6.4))}$$

The additive variance, V_A, is the sum of the variances of the average effects received from the two parents, which are of course equal; the dominance variance, V_D, is the variance of the dominance deviations.

If there is no dominance then of course $V_D = 0$ and all the genetic variance is additive. However, if there is complete dominance it will not usually be true that $V_A = 0$. Consider, for example, the case of two alleles, with frequencies p and $q = 1-p$, when the first allele is completely dominant to the second. It is not difficult to show that

$$V_A/V_D = 2q/p \tag{6.11}$$

Thus when $p = q = \frac{1}{2}$, the additive variance is twice as large as the dominance variance. When p is small nearly all the genetic variance is additive. Only when q, the frequency of the recessive allele, is small does the additive variance become much smaller than the dominance variance.

So far we have only considered the genetic variance contributed by a single locus. If two or more loci act additively in the sense that the total genetic deviation is simply the sum of the genetic deviations at the separate loci, then the variances will also add and Equation (6.4) will remain valid. If, however, there is any interaction between loci whereby the genes at one locus effect the deviation produced by the genes at another locus, then a new cause of genetic variation will be introduced, called the interaction variance, or the epistatic variance, and denoted by V_I. In this case we must write

$$V_G = V_A + V_D + V_I \tag{6.12}$$

It seems likely, however, that the interaction variance will usually be small and can be safely ignored; this course will be adopted here since its treatment is rather complicated. With this proviso, the total variance can be expressed as the sum of three components,

$$V = V_A + V_D + V_E \qquad (6.13)$$

Correlations between relatives

Relatives may resemble each other for two reasons, firstly because they tend to be alike genetically, and secondly because they may tend to share similar environmental circumstances. Consider a pair of related individuals with phenotypic values y and y^*, which may be written

$$y = \mu + g + e$$
$$y^* = \mu + g^* + e^* \qquad (6.14)$$

The covariance of y and y^* is

$$\text{Cov}(y, y^*) = \text{Cov}(g, g^*) + \text{Cov}(e, e^*) \qquad (6.15)$$

The first term on the right-hand side of the above equation reflects the genetic resemblance and the second term the environmental resemblance of the individuals. The environmental covariance may arise in many ways, and is likely to be particularly high in sibs and twins who share similar conditions of upbringing after birth as well as similar intra-uterine conditions before birth. The main purpose of this section, however, is to derive the formula for the genetic covariance of relatives. Before doing this we must consider the concept of *identical genes*.

Two genes are said to be *identical* if one of them has been derived by direct replication from the other. Thus the child of a parent of genotype (a, b) necessarily receives either a or b (never both) from this parent; thus parent and child always have exactly one identical gene in common at each locus. Let us now consider a pair of sibs. Suppose that the father has the genotype (a, b), the mother (c, d), and that the first sib has the genotype (a, c). The second sib is equally likely to have one of the four genotypes (a, c), (a, b), (b, c), or (b, d). In the first case the sibs will have two identical genes, in the second and third cases one identical gene, and in the fourth case no identical genes in common. Hence the probabilities that sibs will have 0, 1, or 2 identical genes in common are $\frac{1}{4}$, $\frac{1}{2}$, and $\frac{1}{4}$ respectively at each locus. The average number of identical genes is one as in the case of parent–child, but the distribution is different. The average number of identical genes held in common will be denoted by I, and the probability that both genes are identical by P. (Readers familiar with population genetics will recognize I as twice Wright's 'coefficient of relationship' and four times Malécot's 'coefficient de parenté'.) Thus we may conclude that for parent–child, $I = 1$, $P = 0$, whereas for sib–sib, $I = 1$, $P = \frac{1}{4}$. The values of I and P can be calculated for other relatives by similar methods but they will not be required in this book.

We are now in a position to consider the genetic correlation between relatives. We shall for the sake of simplicity consider only one locus, but the results can be extended to any number of unlinked loci provided that there is no interaction variance. Consider a pair of related individuals with genotypes (i, j) and (i^*, j^*) and with genetic deviations

$$g = \alpha_i + \alpha_j + d_{ij}$$

$$g^* = \alpha_{i^*} + \alpha_{j^*} + d_{i^*j^*} \qquad (6.16)$$

The genetic covariance is

$$\mathrm{Cov}(g, g^*) = E(gg^*) = E[(\alpha_i + \alpha_j + d_{ij})\,(\alpha_{i^*} + \alpha_{j^*} + d_{i^*j^*})]$$

$$= E(\alpha_i \alpha_{i^*}) + 3 \text{ similar terms}$$

$$+ E(\alpha_i d_{i^*j^*}) + 3 \text{ similar terms}$$

$$+ E(d_{ij} d_{i^*j^*}) \qquad (6.17)$$

Let us now consider these terms in turn. Firstly, if i and $i*$ are identical,

$$E(\alpha_i \alpha_{i*}) = E(\alpha_i^2) = V(\alpha_i) = \tfrac{1}{2}V_A \text{ (from (6.10))}; \quad (6.18)$$

otherwise $E(\alpha_i \alpha_{i*})$ is zero from (6.6). Secondly, $E(\alpha_i d_{i*j*})$ is zero whether or not i is identical with $i*$ or $j*$ from (6.7) and (6.8). Thirdly, if both genes are identical,

$$E(d_{ij} d_{i*j*}) = E(d_{ij}^2) = V_D \text{ (from (6.10))}; \quad (6.19)$$

otherwise $E(d_{ij} d_{i*j*})$ is zero. (When one pair of genes is identical this follows from (6.8)). Hence a contribution of $\tfrac{1}{2}V_A$ is made to the genetic covariance by each pair of identical genes, and a further contribution of V_D is made when both genes are identical. It follows that

$$\mathrm{Cov}(g, g*) = \tfrac{1}{2}IV_A + PV_D \quad (6.20)$$

We can therefore conclude that the genetic covariance between parent and child is $\tfrac{1}{2}V_A$, whereas the genetic covariance between sibs is $\tfrac{1}{2}V_A + \tfrac{1}{4}V_D$.

7 The Use of Twins in Genetic Research

THIS book is primarily concerned with the study of twinning as a subject of interest in its own right, but it would be incomplete without some consideration of the use of twins as tools in genetic research. It was first suggested by Francis Galton in 1875, in a paper on 'The history of twins, as a criterion of the relative powers of nature and nurture', that a comparison of the degree of similarity of monozygotic and dizygotic twins could be used to assess the importance of hereditary and environmental factors in determining human characters. Since that date a large amount of material has been accumulated, but its interpretation has often been rather uncritical and there has in consequence been a recent tendency to stress the limitations of the twin method. There is no doubt that twin material is liable to bias of several kinds and that it needs to be interpreted with caution, but it can nevertheless provide valuable information, particularly when used in conjunction with other types of data. In this chapter we shall try to evaluate the use of the twin method without either minimizing or exaggerating its limitations. We shall begin by considering the analysis of data on quantitative characters such as height.

Quantitative characters

The main tool for investigating the inheritance of quantitative characters is the study of correlations between relatives, and we shall therefore begin by describing briefly how these correlations are measured. The correlation between twins is most easily found by calculating the variances of the difference and of the sum of the paired values observed. If y and y^* are the values of the character in a pair of twins, then

$$V(y-y^*) = V(y)+V(y^*)-2\mathrm{Cov}(y, y^*) = 2V(y)-2\mathrm{Cov}(y, y^*)$$

$$V(y+y^*) = V(y)+V(y^*)+2\mathrm{Cov}(y, y^*) = 2V(y)+2\mathrm{Cov}(y, y^*).$$

If follows that

$$\rho = \frac{\mathrm{Cov}(y, y^*)}{V(y)} = \frac{V(y+y^*)-V(y-y^*)}{V(y+y^*)+V(y-y^*)}.$$

If n pairs of twins have been observed the variances of $(y-y^*)$ and of $(y+y^*)$ can be estimated in the obvious way as

$$V(y-y^*) = \Sigma d^2/n$$

$$V(y+y^*) = (\Sigma s^2 - n\bar{s}^2)/(n-1)$$

where $d = (y-y^*)$ and $s = (y+y^*)$. No correction factor is involved in the calculation of $V(y-y^*)$ since it is assumed that the Expected value of the difference is zero; however, it may be necessary to correct for a sex difference in unlike-sexed twins. The approximate standard errors of these estimates have been given by Kempthorne and Osborne (1961). The correlations are of course calculated separately for monozygotic and dizygotic twins. If an independent estimate is available of the population variance, $V(y)$, the correlation can be estimated from the formula

$$\rho = 1 - \frac{\frac{1}{2}V(y-y^*)}{V(y)}.$$

Results are sometimes quoted in terms of the mean difference between twins, which is related to $V(y-y^*)$, on the assumption of normality, by the formula

$$V(y-y^*) = 1\cdot57(\text{mean difference})^2.$$

If the mean difference between unrelated individuals is also known the correlation can be estimated from the formula

$$\rho = 1 - \frac{(\text{mean difference between twins})^2}{(\text{mean difference between unrelated individuals})^2}.$$

It is customary to calculate the correlation coefficient for parent–child by the ordinary formula for a correlation coefficient, as if all pairs of values were independent. As Holt (1956) points out, this is not strictly true since parent–child pairs from a single family with more than one child are not independent, but it is unlikely that any appreciable error will be introduced other than a slight underestimation of the standard error. The parent–child correlation may equally well be estimated by the regression of child on parent, on the assumption that the variance is the same in both populations. For methods of estimating the sib–sib correlation the reader should consult the paper by Smith (1957).

We must now consider the interpretation of these correlations. It was shown in the Appendix to the last chapter that the total variance of a quantitative character can be split up into a genetic and an environmental component:

$$V = V_G + V_E$$

where V is the total variance, V_G the genetic variance, and V_E the environmental variance. The genetic variance can in turn be divided into an additive component, V_A, and a dominance component, V_D:

$$V_G = V_A + V_D.$$

The significance of these genetic components of variance was discussed in the last chapter. Their importance is that they determine the correlations between relatives. Under random mating and in the absence of genetically determined maternal effects and of epistasis the genetic covariance between parent and child is $\frac{1}{2}V_A$ and the genetic covariance between sibs (or between dizygotic twins) is $\frac{1}{2}V_A + \frac{1}{4}V_D$; the genetic covariance between monozygotic twins is equal to the total genetic variance, V_G, since they are genetically identical. The corresponding correlation coefficients are obtained by dividing these covariances by the total variance, V.

If it can be assumed that the correlations between relatives are entirely of genetic origin they can be used to estimate the relative magnitudes of the three components of variance, V_A, V_D, and V_E. Particular interest lies in estimating the ratio of the genetic variance to the environmental variance which is a measure of the relative importance of nature and nurture, in Francis Galton's phraseology; it is also of interest to find the relative importance of the additive and dominance components of the genetic variance which provides some information about the mode of inheritance.

Unfortunately there are several difficulties in interpreting correlation coefficients between relatives in this way. Firstly, it has been assumed that the character under study has a constant value in any particular individual, whereas many characters, such as height and weight, vary markedly with age; many twin studies have been done on children because of the difficulty of obtaining a sample of adult twins, and the necessity to allow for variation with age is obvious. Some authors, for example Newman, Freeman, and Holzinger (1937) in their classical study of twins, have used a partial correlation eliminating age, but as Fisher (1925) pointed out this is unjustified when the regression on age is not linear, which will usually be the case. A more satisfactory method is to express each observation as a deviation from the mean value of all children of the same age and sex; this deviation should be standardized by dividing it by the standard deviation in the same age and sex group if this standard deviation varies with age or sex. The observations are thus converted into standard scores, like intelligence quotients.

Care must be taken in the interpretation of correlations for age-dependent characters since the correlation may also change with age. For example, it seems likely that the genetic factors which control adult height are not identical with the factors responsible for height in childhood; the parent–child correlation will therefore underestimate the degree of genetic determination and will increase with the age of the child up to its true value (Carter 1962), but the correlation between twins or between sibs of similar age will not be affected in this way. In the case of weight, on the other hand, one would expect to find a higher correlation between twins in childhood than between adult twins because the variability of weight increases with age, probably because of an increase in environmental variability, so that the degree of genetic determination decreases with age. This seems to be the explanation of a discrepancy between the findings of Newman, Freeman and Holzinger (1937) and Shields (1962). Both workers compared a group of monozygotic twins brought up apart with another group brought up together, but Newman found that the separated twins had much larger differences in weight than the unseparated twins, whereas Shields found almost no difference between the two groups. However, most of Newman's separated twins were adult, while all the unseparated twins were children; Shields' twins were almost all adult and were matched for age. It therefore seems likely that Newman's result reflects the difference in age between the two groups rather than the effect of separation.

Another major difficulty of interpretation is that relatives may resemble each other not only because they tend to be alike genetically but also because they may tend to share similar environmental circumstances. Following Falconer (1960) we may divide the environmental variance into two components:

$$V_E = V_{Ec} + V_{Ew}$$

where V_{Ec} is the between-family variance and V_{Ew} is the within-family variance. V_{Ew} is the environmental variance between relatives in the same family and is less than the total environmental variance, V_E, by the amount V_{Ec} which represents the reduction in the environmental variance due to their common environment and which is therefore called the common environmental variance. The covariance between relatives is increased by the amount V_{Ec} in addition to their genetic covariance.

The possible sources of common environmental variance are many, but they may be broadly classed into pre-natal factors due to a similar intra-uterine environment, and post-natal factors due to similar conditions of upbringing during infancy and childhood. The magnitude of the common environmental variance will depend both on the character and on the type of relative under discussion. It is likely to be larger in twins and sibs than between parent and child.

Twins can be used in two ways to overcome the difficulties due to common environmental variance. Firstly, it is sometimes possible to compare monozygotic twins reared apart with monozygotic twins reared together. This is a very valuable method of studying the effect of post-natal environmental differences unobscured by genetic differences, but it may be difficult to obtain from it a precise estimate of the common environmental variance. If it could be assumed that the monozygotic twins reared apart were placed at random in their adopted homes then the correlation between them would reflect only their genetic similarity; but there is always a suspicion that common environmental factors have not been entirely eliminated because of 'selective placement' of the twins in similar homes. For the same reason the correlation between step-sibs, that is to say between unrelated children reared together, may reflect a small amount of genetic similarity in addition to their common environmental variance.

Secondly, it is possible to compare the correlations of monozygotic and dizygotic twins. If it can be assumed that the common environmental variance is the same for the two types of twin, then it will be eliminated by taking the difference between their correlations; we may therefore write

$$2(r_M - r_D) = (V_G + \tfrac{1}{2} V_D)/V$$

where r_M and r_D are the correlations between monozygotic and dizygotic twins respectively. If we can assume that V_D/V is zero, or if an independent estimate of this quantity can be found, we can therefore estimate V_G/V, the proportion of the variance of genetic origin. (It may be noted in passing that the well-known formula of Holzinger (1929), which is equivalent to $(r_M - r_D)/(1 - r_D)$, does not seem so easy to interpret.) However, two objections have been made against the assumption that the common environmental variance is the same for monozygotic and dizygotic twins. Firstly, it has been argued that the environmental difference of monozygotic twins is reduced because they tend to seek similar environments; however, in so far as they do this because of their genetic similarity rather than just to copy one another, their behaviour is a reflection of their genotype and must be regarded as influencing their genetic rather than their environmental variance. Secondly, it has been suggested that the environmental difference between monozygotic twins may be greater than that of dizygotic twins because of the imbalance of the placental circulation sometimes found in monochorial twins (see Chapter 3). It seems likely that the effects of this factor have been exaggerated by critics of the twin method, but this objection could be met by comparing dichorial monozygotic twins with dizygotic twins if information about the placentation of the twins were available.

A third difficulty in interpreting correlations between relatives arises from non-random mating which will inflate the observed correlations if there is a positive correlation between husband and wife. The simplest way of correcting the parent–child correlation for non-random mating is to divide it by $(1+m)$ where m is the husband–wife correlation. This procedure can be justified in two ways. Firstly, it gives the partial regression coefficient in the joint regression of son (or daughter) on both parents simultaneously. (It is assumed that the distributions have been standardized to have the same variance and that the contributions of the two parents, and hence the regression coefficients, are equal.) The calculation of a joint regression is a well-known statistical method for separating the effects of two correlated variables. Secondly, a theoretical investigation of non-random mating by Fisher (1918) and Malécot (1939) has shown that the parent–child correlation can be expressed as

$$(\tfrac{1}{2}V_A/V)\,(1+m)\,(1+e+2e^2+\ \ldots)$$

where

$$e = mV_D V_A/V_G V.$$

If e is small, as will usually be the case, then the parent–child correlation is increased by a factor only slightly larger than $(1+m)$. It can also be shown from the formulae given by Fisher (1918) and Malécot (1939) that the sib–sib, or the dizygotic twin, correlation can be approximately corrected by dividing it by $(1+2rm)$ or by subtracting $2r^2m$ where r is the corrected parent–child correlation. The monozygotic twin correlation does not need to be corrected since the genetic similarity between monozygotic twins is already complete and cannot be increased. The correlations should be corrected for common environmental variance before being corrected for non-random mating. Furthermore, any part of the husband–wife correlation which reflects social rather than genetic factors must be discounted since it will not contribute to the inflation of the genetic similarity between relatives; this is the main practical difficulty in correcting for non-random mating.

We shall now consider some specific examples to see how these difficulties can be overcome in practice. We shall begin by discussing the inheritance of the fingerprint ridge count, which provides a copybook example of what happens in the absence of any complications. A series of familial studies of this character has been carried out by Holt who has summarized her results in two reviews (Holt 1961a, b). The ridges on each finger are counted according to defined rules depending on the fingerprint pattern and are then summed for all ten fingers to give the total ridge count. The correlations between relatives are shown in Table 7.1. It will be observed, firstly that the parent–parent correlation is not significant, so that there is no evidence of non-random mating; secondly, that the mother–child, father–child, sib–sib, and dizygotic twin correlations are very similar and are slightly less than $\frac{1}{2}$, which is the theoretical value when all the variance is additive genetic; and thirdly,

Table 7.1. Correlations between relatives for total fingerprint ridge count
(Holt 1961a, b)

Type of relationship	Correlation coefficient ± standard error
Parent–parent	0·05 ± 0·07
Mother–child	0·48 ± 0·04
Father–child	0·49 ± 0·04
Sib–sib	0·50 ± 0·04
Dizygotic twins	0·49 ± 0·08
Monozygotic twins	0·95 ± 0·01
Left hand–right hand	0·94 ± 0·01

that the monozygotic twin correlation is very high and nearly attains the value of 1 which is its theoretical value when all the variance is of genetic origin.

It can be concluded that there is little or no distortion due to common environmental variance; for any common environmental factor must act pre-natally, since the ridge count is determined by the fourth month of foetal life, and would therefore increase the dizygotic twin and the sib–sib correlation above the parent–child correlation. It can also be concluded that there is little or no dominance component of the genetic variance since the parent–child correlation is as high as the sib–sib and the dizygotic twin correlations.†

† Holt also showed that the regression of the child's ridge count on the mid-parental value is linear and suggested that this provides confirmatory evidence of the absence of dominance. However, if the ridge count is determined by a large number of genetic factors without epistasis then its joint distribution in mother, father, and child must be multivariate normal by the central limit theorem and so all the regressions must be linear whether or not there is dominance.

It therefore seems safe to interpret these data on the assumption that there are no complications due to common environmental variance, assortative mating, or ageing. We can therefore estimate the ratio of genetic variance to total variance as ninety-five per cent from the monozygotic twin correlation. This figure, together with the conclusion that there is no dominance, leads to the prediction that the parent–child and sib–sib correlations should be 0·475, which is very close to their observed values. Confirmation is provided by the very similar figure of 0·94 for the correlation between the two hands of the same individual, although this correlation is not exactly comparable with the correlation between monozygotic twins.

We shall now consider the inheritance of height, which illustrates the difficulties of interpretation which arise from non-random mating and from variation with age. The most extensive and reliable study of the familial correlations for height was published by Pearson and Lee in 1903, who found a parent–child correlation of $0·507\pm0·007$ and a sib–sib correlation of $0·543\pm0·010$. (Following Fisher (1918) I have taken the weighted means, neglecting sex distinctions, which are not significant.) The problem of age-correction does not arise since only adults were included in the sample, but there was a correlation of 0·280 between the heights of husband and wife. This correlation indicates an appreciable degree of non-random mating which is likely to have increased the observed familial correlations. Applying the method of correction described above we find corrected correlations of 0·40 for parent–child and 0·45 for sib–sib.

Data on twins have been reported by several authors, although their interpretation is complicated by considerable variability due to small sample size and by the fact that some of the investigations were done on children. Nevertheless, it can be concluded in general terms that the correlation between dizygotic twins is very similar to the correlation between sibs, but that the correlation between monozygotic twins is much higher and is about 0·95; this figure does not require correction for non-random mating and indicates that about ninety-five per cent of the variability in height is of genetic origin, if it can be assumed that there is no common environmental variance. Two lines of evidence indicate that the latter assumption is at least approximately true. Firstly, there is no correlation between the heights of unrelated children reared together (Burt 1966) and secondly, there is little difference between the correlations of monozygotic twins reared together and apart or between siblings reared together and apart (Newman, Freeman, and Holzinger 1937, Shields 1962, Burt 1966). However, the possibility cannot be ruled out that there is a small degree of common environmental variance between sibs or twins reared together.

If it is assumed that there is no common environmental variance the genetic correlation between relatives (the covariance divided by the genetic variance) can be estimated by dividing the observed correlations, corrected for non-random mating, by 0·95, the correlation between monozygotic twins. The estimated genetic correlations for Pearson and Lee's data are 0·42 for parent–child and 0·47 for sib–sib. If all the genetic variance were additive then both these correlations should be $\frac{1}{2}$, but they will be reduced by the presence of dominance variance, the parent–child correlation being reduced twice as much as the sib–sib correlation. In fact, the reduction in the parent–child correlation is slightly more than twice the reduction in the sib–sib correlation, but the data seem in reasonable agreement with the hypothesis that the dominance variance accounts for about fifteen per cent of the genetic variance; the predicted correlations on this hypothesis are 0·42 for parent–child and 0·46 for sib–sib.

We shall next consider briefly the inheritance of intelligence, which is both the most difficult and the most interesting character to interpret. There is not space here to review the large literature on this controversial subject, but Table 7.2 shows the values of the correlation coefficient which are typically observed; this table has been modified from Table 4 of Burt

(1966) in order to take into account his own results. There is clearly a considerable amount of common environmental variance between children brought up together, since firstly the correlation between monozygotic twins and between sibs drops by about 0·10 when they are reared apart, and secondly there is a correlation of 0·25 between step-sibs. The fact that

Table 7.2. *Typical correlations between relatives for intelligence (modified from* Burt 1966)

Type of relationship	Correlation coefficient
Monozygotic twins reared together	0·88
Monozygotic twins reared apart	0·78
Dizygotic twins reared together	0·55
Sibs reared together	0·55
Sibs reared apart	0·45
Unrelated children reared together	0·25
Parent–child (parent tested as child)	0·56
Husband–wife	0·50

the correlation between step-sibs is greater than the fall in the correlation in sibs reared apart is probably due to selective placement of children in foster homes of comparable socioeconomic level to those of the true parents, which will lead to a small genetic correlation between step-sibs and to a small environmental correlation between sibs reared apart. It therefore seems likely that the common environmental variance between sibs accounts for something between ten per cent and twenty-five per cent of the total variance; for the sake of argument we shall suppose that the true figure is seventeen per cent, and we shall therefore estimate the correlation between monozygotic twins as 0·71 and the correlation between dizygotic twins or sibs as 0·38 after correction for their similar environment.

It will also be seen that there is a high degree of assortative mating, but it seems likely that part of the correlation between husband and wife is environmentally determined through similarity in social class. If we assume that the correlation between husband and wife after eliminating the effect of their common environment would be about 0·3, and if we also assume that twice the parent–child correlation after correction for common environment and assortative mating would be about the same as the corrected correlation between monozygotic twins, then the sib–sib correlation should be divided by about 1·2 to allow for the effect of assortative mating. The corrected value of the correlation between sibs or dizygotic twins obtained in this way is 0·32. If we double this figure it is not far short of the corrected correlation between monozygotic twins. It can be tentatively concluded that about two-thirds of the variability in intelligence is of genetic origin and that there is little or no dominance variance. These conclusions are confirmed by the correlation between parent and child, the parent having been tested in childhood, which is very similar to the sib–sib correlation.

The above estimate of the heritability of intelligence can obviously only be regarded as very approximate. It must also be remembered that the observed correlations between relatives depend both on the tests used (an inaccurate test will produce a low correlation while a 'culturally loaded' test will produce a high correlation due to common environmental factors), and on the homogeneity of the group tested (the more homogeneous the group the smaller will be the range of environmental differences and so the larger the relative influence of heredity). One would therefore expect the relative importance of the genetic contribution to intelligence to increase as increasing equality of educational opportunity leads to a reduction in environmental differences.

We shall finally consider the inheritance of birth weight, which illustrates some rather different points. In many species size at birth is determined largely by the size of the mother and only to a small extent by the genotype of the offspring. For example, when a large Shire horse was crossed with a Shetland pony the weight of the foal of Shire dam and Shetland sire was about the same at birth as that of the foal of pure Shire parents, and the weight of the foal of Shetland dam and Shire sire was no greater than that of the foal of pure Shetland parents (Walton and Hammond 1938); foals from both types of cross eventually grew to a size intermediate between a Shire horse and a Shetland pony. These results indicate that the foal's genotype cannot begin to express itself until after birth since it is overridden by the mother's genotype before birth. Similar, though not so clear-cut, results have been obtained in other species (Joubert and Hammond 1954).

There is a fair amount of evidence, summarized in Table 7.3,

Table 7.3. Correlations between birth weights of surviving infants

Type of relationship	Correlation	Reference
Japanese data		
Full sibs	0·45	Morton 1955
Maternal half-sibs	0·58	,, ,,
Paternal half-sibs	0·10†	,, ,,
Unlike-sexed twins	0·66	,, ,,
Like-sexed twins	0·56	,, ,,
English data		
Full sibs	0·43	Karn, Lang-Brown, MacKenzie, and Penrose 1951
Unlike-sexed twins	0·58	Penrose 1961
Like-sexed twins	0·62	,, ,,
Cousins whose mothers are sisters	0·18	Robson 1955
Other cousins	0·06†	,, ,,
Birth weight and height of mother‡	0·19	McKeown and Record 1954
Birth weight and height of father‡	0·05†	,, ,, ,, ,,

† Not significantly different from zero.
‡ Standardized for the height of the other parent.

that in man birth weight is determined to a considerable extent by the mother and hardly at all by the genotype of the foetus. Thus there is a strong correlation between the birth weights of full sibs and of maternal half-sibs, but little or no correlation between paternal half-sibs; the correlations between like-sexed and unlike-sexed twins are about the same, from which it can be concluded that the correlations between monozygotic and dizygotic twins are also about the same; there is a correlation between the birth weights of cousins whose mothers are sisters, but not between other types of cousins whose related parents are brothers or brother and sister; finally, birth weight is correlated with the height of the mother but not with the father's height. The correlation between cousins whose mothers are sisters indicates that at least part of the influence of the mother on birth weight is hereditary since this corresponds to a sister–sister correlation of the maternal genotypes. We can therefore obtain a rough estimate of the proportion of the variance which is attributable to the maternal genotype (ignoring dominance) as $2 \times 0.18 = 36$ per cent. If we estimate the total proportion of the variance which is attributable to the influence of the mother as about forty-four per cent from the correlation between sibs it will be seen that a large part of this maternally determined variance is hereditary. The remaining fifty-six per cent of the variance must be attributed to accidental causes unrelated either to the constitution of the mother or to the foetal genotype. These estimates must of course only be regarded as very approximate.

We must now examine more critically the correlations between twins. It will be observed that the correlation between unlike-sexed twins is higher than the correlation between sibs, and it has been suggested by Penrose (1961) that this difference can be used to estimate the effect of the immediate maternal environment which affects foetuses in the same pregnancy but not in subsequent pregnancies. However, twins have almost exactly the same length of gestation, whereas sibs do not; this factor alone will increase the correlation between twins since birth weight is correlated with length of gestation. Indeed, it is likely that the figures in Table 7.3 underestimate the difference between sibs and twins since they are based on surviving infants only, stillbirths and neonatal deaths being excluded in order to eliminate abnormal foetuses. If all births are included, the correlation coefficient for twins rises to about 0·7 (Karn 1952, 1953, Fraccaro 1957); there might also be a similar rise for sibs, but it would be less since fewer non-survivors have been excluded. It would seem unwise to place much reliance on the difference between the correlations of twins and sibs for a character such as birth weight on which twinning itself has a large effect.

The other comparison of interest is between monozygotic and dizygotic twins. It has already been remarked that the correlations between like-sexed and unlike-sexed twins are about the same, which lends support to the supposition that the foetal genotype has little influence on birth weight, but care must be taken in interpreting the correlation between monozygotic twins which may well be affected by the fact that about two-thirds of them are monochorial. In the first place, the imbalance of the placental circulation in some monochorial twins can lead to marked differences in birth weight, which will depress the correlation of monozygotic twins. On the other hand, the fact that monochorial twins are on average about half a pound lighter than dichorial twins, as was shown in Chapter 3, will tend to increase the apparent correlation of monozygotic twins when the two chorial types are grouped together. It is clearly necessary to consider monochorial and dichorial monozygotic twins separately and to compare the correlation of dichorial monozygotic twins with that of dizygotic twins in order to obtain a meaningful result. It should not be too difficult to obtain data on the birth weights of twins classified simultaneously by sex and chorial type, but at present no adequate body of published data is available.

Concordance and discordance

Many traits of genetic interest are either present or absent in an individual. We shall usually be thinking of a pathological trait, such as clubfoot or diabetes, and we shall therefore describe individuals with the trait as affected and individuals without the trait as unaffected or normal. In this account we shall ignore the difficulties which arise from variations in the degree of severity and in the age of onset of many diseases, although allowance can be made for the latter.

If both twins of a pair are affected they are said to be concordant for the trait, while if one twin is affected and the other normal they are said to be discordant; we shall not here be concerned with the third class of twins who are concordant for the absence of the trait. The frequency of concordance can be defined in several different ways (Allen, Harvald and Shields 1967), but the most useful method is to define it as the proportion of affected individuals among the co-twins of previously defined index cases; this has been called the proband concordance rate by Allen, Harvald, and Shields (1967), since it is obtained by the application of the proband method of Weinberg, treating twin pairs as sibships of two (Weinberg 1928, Bailey 1961). The estimate of concordance from the observed numbers of concordant and discordant pairs will depend on the number of concordant pairs in whom both affected individuals were independently ascertained index patients since these pairs must be counted twice. The frequency of concordance is therefore estimated from the formula:

$$\text{concordance} = \frac{c + 2c^*}{c + 2c^* + d}$$

where c is the number of concordant pairs ascertained through only one of the affected twins, c^* is the number of concordant pairs ascertained independently through both affected twins, and d is the number of discordant pairs. If the chance of ascertaining an affected twin is small (this is usually referred to as single ascertainment) then c^* will be zero and the above formula reduces to the conventional formula

$$\text{concordance} = c/(c + d).$$

If, on the other hand, an attempt is made to ascertain all

affected twins in the population (this is usually referred to as complete ascertainment), then c will be zero and the formula becomes

$$\text{concordance} = 2c^*/(2c^*+d)$$

which is considerably higher than the conventional formula, which ignores the effect of the method of ascertainment on the expected frequency of concordant pairs. It is sometimes difficult to decide whether a pair of concordant twins have been independently ascertained or not and it is therefore preferable to attempt complete ascertainment if this is practical. It is dangerous to rely on case reports collected from the literature which are liable to be biased by the inclusion of too many concordant pairs.

There are two advantages in using the proband concordance rate defined above. Firstly, it can be compared directly with the incidence of the disease in the general population or in other relatives of affected individuals; for example, the concordance in dizygotic twins should be the same as the incidence among siblings of affected individuals, provided that being a twin does not affect the chance of having the disease, since siblings are genetically as alike as dizygotic twins. Secondly, the proband concordance rate in monozygotic twins can be interpreted as a weighted average penetrance, provided that the incidence of the disease is unaffected either by being a monozygotic twin or by environmental factors common to twin pairs; the latter assumption is unfortunately often unjustified. Let us suppose that the above assumptions are true and that there are several genotypes which affect the chance of getting the disease. We shall suppose that an individual with the ith genotype has a chance p_i of developing the disease (this is called the penetrance of the genotype), and that the population frequency of this genotype is π_i. Hence the probability that an affected individual will have the ith genotype is $\pi_i p_i / \Sigma \pi_i p_i$, and so the probability that the monozygotic co-twin of an affected individual will also be affected, which is the expected concordance in monozygotic twins, is

$$\Sigma\pi_i p_i^2 \big| \Sigma\pi_i p_i.$$

(These results follow from the Bayesian argument used in the last chapter in connection with the repeat frequency of twinning.)

The above quantity can be interpreted as a weighted average of the penetrances where each penetrance is weighted not by π_i but by $\pi_i p_i$, the product of its probability and of its own value. This is rather an odd sort of average, but it does have some intuitive meaning and can be used to test specific genetic hypotheses. Alternatively, if we regard the penetrance, p, as the quantity which is inherited, the above formula can be written in the form

$$C = \frac{E(p^2)}{P} = \frac{V(p) + P^2}{P}$$

where C is the concordance between monozygotic twins, P is the population incidence of the disease, and $V(p)$ is the genetic variance of p, which also includes any common environmental variance. It follows that

$$V(p) = P(C - P).$$

It can be shown in a similar way that, if R is the incidence of the disease in the relatives of an affected person, the genetic covariance between these relatives, including again any common environmental variance, can be estimated as $P(R - P)$. It follows that the genetic correlation between relatives can be estimated as $(R - P)/(C - P)$, if it can be assumed that there is no common environmental variance.

As an example we shall consider the inheritance of congenital malformations. In a recent review Carter (1965) has shown that the family patterns of the four best-documented malformations (harelip, congenital dislocation of the hip, clubfoot, and pyloric stenosis) are similar. There are differences in detail, and complications arise from differences in the degree of severity of the malformation, from differential incidence in the two sexes, and from deficiencies in the data. Instead of analysing the data for a particular malformation we shall therefore consider an idealized 'typical' malformation with the following pattern of inheritance: (1) the population incidence is about one per thousand; (2) the concordance in monozygotic twins is about fifty per cent; (3) the concordance in dizygotic twins and the incidence in siblings and children of affected individuals is about three and a half per cent; (4) the incidence in second-degree relatives (aunts, uncles, nephews, and nieces) of affected individuals is about five per thousand; (5) the incidence in third-degree relatives (first cousins) of affected individuals is about two per thousand. The genetic correlations for penetrance between first-, second-, and third-degree relatives calculated from the formula in the previous paragraph are 0·07, 0·008, and 0·002 respectively.

These correlations are very much lower than those predicted by the theory of quantitative genetics outlined in the previous section and in the last chapter. The fact that the incidence is as high among children as among siblings of affected individuals shows that there is no dominance variance, and we should therefore expect the genetic correlations between first-, second-, and third-degree relatives to be $\frac{1}{2}$, $\frac{1}{4}$, and $\frac{1}{8}$ respectively. It is possible that the concordance in monozygotic twins has been inflated by the fact that the incidence of congenital malformations is about twice as high in monozygotic twins as in the general population (see Chapter 3), but it seems unlikely that this has had a large effect, nor would it explain why the correlation is nine times rather than twice as high in first-degree as in second-degree relatives. The only plausible explanation is that there is a high degree of interaction between genes at different loci. The effect of such interaction has so far been ignored, but if it exists it will give rise to a new source of genetic variance, the interaction variance, sometimes called the epistatic variance, which reduces the correlations between relatives. If all the genetic variance is additive, the genetic variance can be written as

$$V_G = V_A + V_{AA} + V_{AAA} + \cdots$$

where V_A is the additive genetic variance, V_{AA} is the interaction variance arising from interactions between the additive effects of genes at two loci, and so on. It can be shown (Kempthorne 1955) that the genetic covariance between n^{th}-degree relatives is

$$(\tfrac{1}{2})^n V_A + (\tfrac{1}{4})^n V_{AA} + (\tfrac{1}{8})^n V_{AAA} + \cdots$$

To explain the estimated correlations it must be supposed that most of the genetic variance arises from high-order interactions, and that at least four loci are involved since the correlation between first-degree relatives is approximately equal to $\frac{1}{16}$.

A genetic model in which most of the genetic variance arises from high-order interactions is perfectly valid but it is not very useful or illuminating. Considerable success has been obtained with an alternative model in which it is supposed that the presence or absence of a trait such as a congenital malformation, is determined by an underlying continuous variable, X, and that an individual is affected only if X exceeds some threshold value, T. It may be supposed that X is normally distributed and has been standardized to have zero mean and unit variance. The value of the threshold can therefore be calculated from the population incidence of the disease, P; for example, if $P = 0\cdot001$, as is the case for the 'typical' congenital malformation considered above, then we must suppose that $T = 3\cdot09$, which is the upper $0\cdot1$ per cent point of the normal distribution. Furthermore, if we denote the values of the underlying variable in a pair of relatives by X and X^*, and if the incidence of the disease in relatives of affected individuals is R, then

$$\text{Prob}\,[X^* > T \,|\, X > T] = R$$

from which it follows that

$$\text{Prob}[X > T \text{ and } X^* > T] = PR.$$

If we assume that X and X^* follow a bivariate normal distribution with correlation ρ, which is equivalent to the assumption that the regression of X^* on X is linear with coefficient ρ, then ρ can be determined by interpolation in tables of the bivariate normal distribution. This technique is known to statisticians as tetrachoric correlation. Appropriate tables will be found in Pearson (1931), National Bureau of Standards (1959), and Owen (1962), although Pearson's tables do not cover threshold values above 2·6.†

If the above method is applied to the 'typical' data for congenital malformations previously quoted it will be found that the correlation for monozygotic twins is 0·92 and that the correlations for first-, second-, and third-degree relatives are 0·43, 0·22, and 0·08 respectively. These are the phenotypic correlations for the hypothetical underlying variable. If the correlation for monozygotic twins is taken at its face value as indicating that ninety-two per cent of the variability in the underlying variable is of genetic origin, then the genetic correlations for other relatives can be obtained by dividing the calculated values by 0·92; the resulting estimated genetic correlations for first-, second-, and third-degree relatives are respectively 0·47, 0·24, and 0·09. These values are very close to the theoretical values of $\frac{1}{2}$, $\frac{1}{4}$, and $\frac{1}{8}$ predicted on the assumption that all the genetic variance is additive and that there is no interaction between different loci. Alternatively, the correlation

---

† It should be noted that this method does not give the same result as the method proposed by Falconer (1965). The latter method is based on the assumptions that the conditional distribution of X^*, given that $X > T$, is normal with unit variance and that only the mean of the distribution changes; the assumptions both of normality and of unit variance are false if X and X^* are bivariate normal, except in the trivial case of zero correlation. Furthermore, Falconer's method leads to nonsense results when applied to high concordances in monozygotic twins; for example, if the population incidence is one per cent, Falconer's method gives a correlation greater than one if the concordance is greater than sixty-seven per cent; there seems no reason why the concordance should not take any value up to one hundred per cent. These deficiencies have been recognized by Falconer (1967). It is therefore suggested that the method of tetrachoric correlation should be used instead, although the calculations involved are rather more tedious.

for first-degree relatives can be doubled to give an estimate of the percentage of genetic variability; this gives a figure of eighty-six per cent, only slightly less than the figure calculated from monozygotic twins. It can be concluded that the threshold model is successful, that the underlying variable behaves genetically like a straightforward continuous character without dominance or recessivity and without epistasis, and that about ninety per cent of its variability is of genetic origin.

It has been assumed so far that the resemblance between relatives is due entirely to their genetic similarity and is unaffected by common environmental factors. In many cases this assumption is unjustified. As an example we shall consider the data of Kallmann and Reisner (1943) shown in Table 7.4

Table 7.4. The incidence of tuberculosis among relatives of tuberculous twins (Kallmann and Reisner 1943)

Relationship to tuberculous twin	Cases of tuberculosis	Number in group over 14 years old	Percentage affected
Unrelated general population	—	—	1·1
Husband or wife	14	226	7·2
Parent	114	688	16·6
Half-sib	4	42	9·5
Full sib	136	720	18·9 ⎱ 18·7
Dizygotic co-twin	42	230	18·3 ⎰
Monozygotic co-twin	48	78	61·5

on the incidence of tuberculosis among relatives of tuberculous twins.† The fact that the concordance is much higher in monozygotic than in dizygotic twins strongly suggests that resistance

† In their original paper, Kallmann and Reisner (1943) corrected for differences in the age of onset of the disease by the abridged Weinberg method which attempts to allow for relatives who are normal at the time of study but who may develop the disease later. It seems likely, however, that this method will over-correct, and in particular will lead to an inflated concordance in monozygotic twins, because the age of onset in relatives is correlated. I have therefore used the crude incidence, uncorrected for age of onset.

to tuberculosis is genetically controlled, but it is also likely that both resistance and exposure to infection will be influenced by socio-economic factors which are shared by members of the same family. We shall now consider how allowance can be made for these common environmental factors on the assumption that the threshold model is valid.

The observed concordance of 61·5 per cent in monozygotic twins together with a population incidence of 1·1 per cent, which corresponds to a threshold of 2·3, leads to an estimated tetrachoric correlation of about 0·93. Likewise, the concordance of 18·7 per cent in dizygotic twins, calculated from the combined data for dizygotic twins and full sibs, gives a tetrachoric correlation of 0·59. The fact that the latter correlation is greater than $\frac{1}{2}$ can be explained by the effect of common environmental factors. If it is assumed that the effect of these factors is the same in monozygotic and dizygotic twins the proportion of the variance attributable to genetic factors can be estimated as $2 \times (0·93 - 0·59) = 68$ per cent; it follows that the proportion of the variance due to common environmental factors is 25 per cent, and the proportion due to other environmental factors 7 per cent. On this model the correlation between second-degree relatives (e.g. half-sibs) should be $0·25 + \frac{1}{4} \times 0·68 = 0·42$, which leads to a predicted incidence of 9·8 per cent among half-sibs of affected individuals; and the correlation between unrelated individuals in the same family (e.g. step-sibs) should be 0·25, which leads to a predicted incidence of 4·6 per cent among step-sibs of affected individuals.

An alternative method is to assume that the effect of the common environmental factors is to lower the threshold among relatives of affected individuals, and to calculate the tetrachoric correlations from this modified threshold. The ideal procedure would be to determine the threshold from the incidence among step-sibs of affected individuals, but in the absence of this information it seems reasonable to assume a threshold which gives twice as large a tetrachoric correlation for monozygotic as for dizygotic twins. By trial and error I found that a threshold of 1·8, which corresponds to an incidence among step-sibs of affected individuals of 3·6 per cent, gives tetrachoric correlations of 0·45 and 0·90 in dizygotic and monozygotic twins; the predicted incidence in half-sibs of affected individuals is 9·1 per cent. It should be observed that this method absorbs the common environmental variance in the reduction of the threshold and does not count it as part of the variance of the underlying variable. If we wish to estimate the genetic variance as a proportion of the total variance, including the common environmental variance, we can do so from the formula $r(1-r^*)/(1-r)$, where r is the tetrachoric correlation in monozygotic twins just calculated and r^* is the tetrachoric correlation found by calculating the threshold from the incidence in the general population. Substituting the observed values of $r = 0·90$, $r^* = 0·93$, in this formula we find that the genetic variance accounts for about sixty-three per cent of the total variance; this is in reasonable agreement with the figure found in the preceding paragraph. It should be borne in mind, however, that these calculations depend heavily on the assumptions that the threshold model is correct and that all the genetic variance is additive. (The fact that the incidence of tuberculosis is slightly lower among parents than among sibs of affected twins does not necessarily indicate the existence of dominance variance; it might be due, for example, to the fact that tuberculous individuals have fewer children because they die younger or to a lower degree of common environmental variance between parent and child than between sibs.)

In conclusion, therefore, the threshold model allows us to convert concordances and incidences into correlations and hence to analyse discontinuous characters as if they were continuous; for this reason Grüneberg (1952), who pointed out the value of the threshold model in animal genetics, has described such characters as 'quasi-continuous'. Examples of other diseases which can be usefully treated by this method are diabetes mellitus (Falconer 1967) and schizophrenia. (The extensive literature on twin studies of schizophrenia has been reviewed by Gottesman and Shields (1966), although the concordances are calculated by the conventional rather than by the proband method.) It is possible to introduce further refinements into the analysis. For example, it can be postulated that different degrees of severity of a disease correspond to different thresholds, or that a different incidence in the two sexes is due to a sex difference in the threshold; these postulates lead to verifiable predictions about the incidence of disease in relatives of affected persons when both the relatives and the index cases are broken down by degree of severity or by sex. There seems no doubt that the threshold model will prove a valuable tool in the analysis of the genetics of discontinuous characters in man.

8 The Evolutionary Significance of Twinning

THE most obvious fact about twins is that they are exceptions to the general rule that the normal human litter size is one. In this chapter we shall try to discover how natural selection may have led to the evolution of single births in man and what role this factor may have played in the evolution of the human species. To set the problem in its proper context we shall first consider in general the evolutionary factors which have determined litter size in mammals, and we shall then discuss in more detail the evolution of litter size in the primates, before we study the selective forces which may be at work in controlling the reproductive rate of the human species.

The evolution of litter size in mammals

It is likely that the lower vertebrates, fish, amphibia, and reptiles, which take little or no care of their young after the eggs are laid, lay as many eggs as they are physiologically capable of producing. There is of course an enormous variation in the number of eggs laid by different species; some fish, such as the cod, may lay several million eggs, whereas the little skate lays only half a dozen. However, there is a high correlation between the number of eggs laid and the size of the egg; fish tend to lay either a large number of small or a small number of large eggs. Thus the egg of the prolific cod is under 1 mm in diameter, while that of a skate is about one hundred times as large; since the volume of an egg is proportional to the cube of its diameter, a million cod eggs are roughly equivalent in volume to a single skate egg, and the total volume of eggs produced by these two fish is about the same.

We may therefore suppose that, with a given food intake, a species can only produce a fixed volume of eggs, which may be composed of a large number of small eggs or a small number of large eggs. Now the large eggs of fish like the skate are rich in food material (yolk) on which the embryo can develop to an advanced stage before hatching and are protected from predators by a horny shell, whereas the small eggs of fish like the cod contain almost no yolk, so that the embryo must hatch soon after fertilization when the loss from predation will be enormous. The low mortality of large eggs is an obvious selective advantage, which is counterbalanced by the fact that only a small number of them can be produced. It is postulated that in a particular species the compromise between these two factors which has actually evolved through natural selection is that which leads to the largest number of offspring which survive to reproduce in the next generation.

It therefore seems likely that nearly all the cold-blooded vertebrates lay as many eggs as they are capable of producing and that the number of eggs laid depends mainly on the size of the egg; for a given expenditure of energy a species may invest in a large number of small eggs with a high mortality, or in a small number of large, better-equipped eggs with a low mortality. In each species the compromise reached will be that which leads to the maximum number of surviving offspring. But in the higher, warm-blooded vertebrates, the birds and mammals, which care for their young after birth, another factor must be taken into account.

It is clear that a bird does not produce as many eggs as it can; for if the eggs are taken during laying it will usually lay more and can be made to lay a much larger number of eggs than usual in this way. To explain the evolution of clutch size in birds, Lack (1954, 1966) has argued that the parents can only provide a limited amount of food for the nestlings and that above some limiting optimal size, large clutches will have fewer survivors per brood than smaller clutches because of the increased mortality from undernourishment; the normal clutch size will therefore evolve through natural selection towards this optimal size which produces the largest number of adult survivors. Lack has provided convincing evidence of the truth of this thesis in birds; his data on survival in relation to brood size in swifts are reproduced in Table 8.1. When it is borne in

Table 8.1. Survival in relation to brood size in swifts (Lack 1954)

Brood size	Number of young hatched	Per cent flying	Young raised per brood
Alpine swift (*Apus melba*) in Switzerland			
1	58	97	1·0
2	562	87	1·8
3	1623	79	2·4
4	20	60	2·4
Common swift (*Apus apus*) in England			
1	36	83	0·8
2	204	84	1·7
3	96	58	1·7

mind that there is considerable mortality after the young have left the nest, which is also likely to depend on brood size, it is almost certain that the optimal brood size is three in the Alpine swift and two in the common swift; these are also the most usual brood sizes.

In mammals, mortality is likely to be higher in large than in small litters, both because the mother is able to take less individual care of the young after birth and because they will be born younger and more helpless; in addition there may well be increased maternal mortality due to the physical strain and disability placed on the mother both before and after birth. We shall therefore assume as a working hypothesis that for each species of mammal there is an optimal litter size which leads on the average to the largest number of surviving offspring, and that the actual litter size typical of the species tends to evolve towards this optimal size through natural selection.

It has been suggested that litter size has adjusted itself through natural selection to balance the natural mortality of the species. On this view it is supposed, for example, that the rabbit has large litters to offset its high mortality, whereas the elephant with its much longer expectation of life need have only one young at a time in order to survive; it might further be suggested that, if elephants had large litters, they would be in danger of over-running Africa and ultimately of becoming extinct through starvation. However, this theory is based on a false view of natural selection. If some elephants have a hereditary predisposition to produce twins, and if these elephants on the average produce a larger number of offspring which survive to reproductive age, then the proportion of twin-producing elephants will increase from one generation to the next until eventually all elephants will have twins, regardless of whether this is to the ultimate benefit of the species. The fact that elephants usually have single births therefore suggests that one is the optimal litter size and that twin-producing elephants would leave fewer surviving descendants than elephants which produce only one young at a time. It is undoubtedly a fact that species with a low mortality tend to have smaller litters than those with a high mortality. But this does not 'explain' the evolution of litter size; it is simply a reflection of the fact that most natural populations are relatively stable in size, and that their birth-rate must therefore be equal to their death-rate.

The most successful general theory of the evolution of litter size was put forward rather briefly by the anatomist Frederic Wood Jones in his book *Arboreal Man* published in 1916, in which he discussed the influence of the arboreal habit in the evolution of man; fuller accounts of his theory are contained in two articles, the first published in 1915 and the second thirty years later in 1945. Wood Jones' thesis was that the terrestrial insectivores from which the primates evolved had large litters, but that the adoption of an arboreal mode of life by the primates led, among other things, to a reduction in litter size because of the difficulty of producing and caring for a large litter up a tree. This difficulty can be overcome to some extent by building a nest, as is done for example by squirrels, but this solution becomes very inconvenient for larger species; in most primates the problem has been solved by reducing the litter to a single offspring which can be carried around on the mother's back or under her belly.

In generalizing his theory to other mammalian orders, Wood Jones argued that litter size is reduced under two circumstances: firstly, in mammals in which the females are highly active during pregancy, and secondly in mammals whose habits and environment prevent them from having a natural nursery in which the offspring may be tended by the mother. Thus all marine mammals (whales, dolphins, and seals) produce only a single young. The difficulties of nursing the young in the sea are obvious, and it is thus advantageous for the young to be born at as advanced a stage as possible and for the gestation period to be long and the lactation period short; this requires a reduction in the number of young. Similarly, defenceless animals like horses which live in open spaces and escape from danger by flight cannot afford to be pregnant with a large litter (since this would prevent the mother from running) or to bear young in a helpless, premature stage. Lastly, flying animals, like bats, which carry the young with them as they fly in search of food must reduce the number of offspring for the same reasons as arboreal mammals. Wood Jones summarizes his argument by saying: 'It is only the strong and the well armed, or such of the weak and defenceless as happen to have homes and safe retreats in lairs or holes or burrows or nests that can afford large litters that they may nurse and tend in safety and at their leisure'.

Wood Jones' theory is biologically plausible and accounts for many of the differences in litter size in mammals. It also provides a partial explanation of the small litter size of most large mammals, since only small mammals can seek protection in nests or burrows; but it is likely that there is an additional reason for this fact. It is well known that the weight of an animal is proportional to the cube of its linear dimensions, while the weight-bearing strength of its bones depends on their cross-sectional area and is thus proportional only to the square of their dimensions; hence the limbs of an elephant must be disproportionately thick compared with those of a small mammal in order to support its weight. In the same way it may be suggested that a large mammal will be reproductively less efficient than a small one, and will in consequence be forced to reduce the number of young which it can bear at a time, because the nourishment of the foetus takes place across the placenta which has a surface area proportional to the square of its linear dimensions, while the volume of nourishment required by the foetus is proportional to the cube of its dimensions. There may well be other factors of a similar, dimensional kind which predispose large mammals to have small litters. This argument is supported by the fact that the relative weight of the litter compared with that of the mother decreases as the size of the species increases, varying from about forty per cent in bats and small rodents to about five per cent in the large mammals (Leitch, Hytten, and Billewicz 1959).

In conclusion, it is postulated that mortality, both of the young and of the mother, increases with the size of the litter, and that in consequence there is an optimal litter size which on average leads to the largest number of surviving offspring. This optimal size, towards which the actual litter size characteristic of the species will tend through natural selection, will be small in mammals in which the females are highly active during pregnancy and in mammals whose way of life does not allow them to have a nursery in which the young can be tended by the mother; the reduction of litter size in the primates can thus be attributed to their adoption of an active, arboreal way of life. It is also likely that the optimal litter size will be lower in large mammals because they are reproductively less efficient for dimensional reasons. With these considerations in mind we shall now discuss in more detail the evolution of litter size in the primates.

Litter size in the primates

It is generally thought that the Primates, the order of mammals to which man belongs, have developed over the course of about a hundred million years from primitive mammals resembling the modern tree-shrews of south-east Asia (Le Gros Clark 1962). Living primates can be divided into two main groups, the pre-monkeys or prosimians (Suborder Prosimii) and the monkeys proper (Suborder Anthropoidea). The prosimians are the more primitive group and include the tree-shrews, the lemurs, now confined to Madagascar, the lorises of tropical Africa and Asia, the African bushbabies, and the Asiatic tarsiers; the tree-shrews are more primitive than other prosimians and their inclusion among the primates is not universally accepted. The more advanced suborder of Anthropoidea includes the New World and Old World monkeys, the anthropoid apes (gorilla, chimpanzee, orangutan, and gibbon), and man himself.

The primates are difficult to define as an order because they have remained rather unspecialized, but they are marked by several characteristics which are associated with their arboreal way of life. One adaptation to arboreal life is the development of hands and feet which can grasp branches by the opposition of the thumb or big toe to the other digits, together with the replacement of claws by nails. Another adaptation is the development of vision at the expense of smell; the reduction in the sense of smell has led to a reduction in the muzzle and a fore-shortening of the face, while the development of visual acuity has led to an increase in the size of the eyes together with a rotation from a lateral position to a position in the front of the head which permits binocular vision. Corresponding changes have also occurred in the brain. But the adaptation which particularly concerns us here is in the pattern of reproduction.

Most small mammals have several offspring in a litter; the young are born in a helpless condition and are cared for by the mother in a nest which they do not leave for some time after birth. This pattern of reproduction is found today in tree-shrews and in one group of Madagascan lemurs (Cheirogaleinae), and it seems likely that it represents the primitive condition among the ancestors of the primates. However, most living primates have developed a pattern of reproduction in which a single offspring is born at a more advanced stage of development and clings to the mother from birth. The essential feature of this pattern is that the young are not left alone in a nest but accompany their mother when she goes out in search of food. The advantages of this behaviour are that it gives greater protection to the young and greater freedom of movement to the parents since they are not tied to the nest. However, it places a strong limitation on the number of young which can be successfully reared since it would be difficult for the mother to carry several offspring on her body, and since it necessitates a longer length of gestation to allow the young to be active enough at birth to cling to their mother; both these factors favour a reduction in litter size. With this general pattern in mind we shall now review the available evidence about litter size and nursing behaviour in the various groups of primates. The reader is referred to Napier and Napier (1967) for authority for most of the following information, when other authority is not cited.

Tree-shrews. Twins or triplets are usual in nearly all species. The young are born hairless and with closed eyes after about one and a half months' gestation, compared with four to five months in most prosimians. They are reared in a separate nest from the mother and are only visited and fed by her once every forty-eight hours (Martin 1966). Apart from the latter rather curious specialization these most primitive primates exhibit the typical primitive pattern of reproduction.

Madagascan lemurs. The dwarf lemurs *(Cheirogaleus)* and the mouse lemurs *(Microcebus)*, which belong to the same subfamily

(Cheirogaleinae), have a primitive pattern of reproduction. They usually have twins or triplets and the young are born in a helpless condition with closed eyes after two to two and a half months' gestation. They are reared in a nest of leaves or in the hollow of a tree, and they may be picked up in the mother's month but do not cling to her. In all other Madagascan lemurs single births are the rule, and most of them have the typical advanced pattern of reproduction: the young are born in an active state with open eyes and covered with hair after four to five months' gestation, they cling to the mother from birth and are carried around by her all the time. This description is certainly true of *Lemur macaco, Lemur fulvus, Lemur catta*, and *Propithecus verreauxi* (Rand 1935, Petter-Rousseaux 1964), but in the nocturnal sportive lemur (*Lepilemur mustelinus*) the young stays behind on a small branch or in the hollow of a tree while the mother forages at night, and in the ruffed lemur (*Lemur variegatus*) the single young is born helpless (the length of gestation is unknown), is reared in a nest made from the mother's fur, and never learns to cling to her (Petter-Rousseaux 1964). It is significant that the primitive pattern of reproduction is found in the Cheirogaleinae which are in some other respects the most primitive, as well as the smallest, of the Madagascan lemurs, but the retention of the primitive nursing behaviour by the ruffed lemur alone in its genus is rather puzzling.

Bushbabies. Bushbabies are arboreal, nocturnal creatures which leap through the trees with great agility. They spend the day in small groups in nests made in tree-holes, or sometimes in African beehives. The young are born in these nests in a fairly advanced stage of development after about five months' gestation and are capable of clinging to their mother from birth. However, they do not accompany the mother but remain behind in the nest when she goes out at night. These facts suggest that bushbabies once possessed a typical advanced pattern of reproduction but have subsequently reverted to rearing their young in nests; the reasons for this evolutionary reversion are unknown but it may be connected with their prodigious leaping, which might be encumbered by the presence of offspring, or by their nocturnal habits.

Some confusion has arisen about litter size in bushbabies from failure to realize that there are differences between different subspecies of the same species. In the common bush-baby, *Galago senegalensis*, twins are usual in the Moholi sub-species, *G. s. moholi*, found in South Africa, but single births are the rule in other subspecies and in particular in the nominal subspecies, *G. s. senegalensis* (Hollister 1924, Lowther 1940, Brand 1963, Haddow and Ellice 1964, Butler 1967, Doyle, Pelletier, and Bekker 1967). In the larger thick-tailed bush-baby, *Galago crassicaudatus*, single births are the rule in most subspecies, but there is some evidence that twins may be common in the silvery bushbaby, *G. c. argentatus* (Buettner-Janusch 1964). These subspecific differences are of great interest in view of the suggestion that bushbabies have reverted secondarily to rearing their young in nests, and it may be suggested that they are consequently in the process of evolving back again from single to multiple births.

Lorises and pottos. The lorises of Asia and the pottos of Africa are nocturnal creatures which move with great deliberation as if in slow motion. They have a typical advanced pattern of reproduction, the young being born at a fairly advanced stage after about five months' gestation, and clinging to the mother as she ambulates through the trees. Single births are the rule, but there is some evidence that twins may be common in the Mysore subspecies of the slender loris, *Loris tardigradus lydekkerianus*.

Tarsiers. The rather rare tarsiers of south-east Asia are small, nocturnal creatures, noted for leaping rather like bush-babies. They do not have nests and their pattern of reproduc-tion is the typical advanced pattern. Single births are the rule.

New World monkeys. The New World monkeys are divided into two families, the marmosets (Callithricidae = Hapalidae) and the Cebidae. Marmosets are in general smaller than the Cebidae, have claws instead of nails, except on the big toe, and have two molar teeth in each half jaw instead of three. They also differ in litter size, single births being the rule in Cebidae and twins in marmosets. In both families the young are born in a fairly mature stage after about five months' gestation. In most Cebidae the infant clings at first to the mother's belly and later to her back, but in titis (*Callicebus*) the infant is carried by the father except when it is being fed by the mother; the father also plays a part in carrying the infant in douroucoulis (*Aoutus*) and in squirrel monkeys (*Saimiri*). In marmosets the young are invariably carried by the father from very soon after birth and are only received by the mother for short periods for suckling. The production of twins by marmosets is probably an evolutionary reversal rather than a primitive character since they possess a unicornuate uterus and a single pair of nipples which are adaptations correlated with single births. It may be suggested that the production of twins has evolved because of their small size and squirrel-like movement; the paternal care of the offspring may also be relevant.

Old World monkeys and anthropoid apes. Single births are the rule in all species. The young are born after about six months' gestation in monkeys and seven to nine months in apes. They cling to the mother's belly and, unlike New World monkeys, they are not usually carried on her back, at least until they are quite old. In some of the Colobus monkeys, however, the infant is carried in its mother's mouth for several weeks after birth before it is transferred to her belly where it is self-supporting; it has been suggested that this behaviour is due to the absence of the thumb in these monkeys, which makes clinging more difficult. In many species the infant is supported by the mother's arm or hand when she is sitting or moving rapidly; this behaviour is not found in prosimians, in which the young are left to cling unsupported.

It can be concluded that the primitive pattern of reproduction, in which several young are born in a helpless condition and are cared for by the mother in a nest, is found today in tree-shrews and in one subfamily of Madagascan lemurs. Most other primates have developed a more advanced pattern of reproduction in which a single infant is born in a more advanced stage after a longer gestational period, and clings to its mother from birth. However, the bushbabies have reverted to rearing their young in nests, and the marmosets to producing twins, for reasons which are only partly understood. We will now consider briefly what effect the change in the pattern of reproduction has had on other aspects of primate evolution.

The reduction of litter size in primates has led both to anatomical changes in the reproductive system and to functional changes in the pattern of reproduction. The main anatomical changes are the development of an undivided, unicornuate uterus and the reduction in the number of mammae to the single pair found in all higher primates. Most mammals have a paired, or bicornuate, uterus in which two long horns meet in a small common chamber, the body of the uterus, which opens into the vagina; the embryos develop in the uterine horns. This type of uterus is found in all prosimians, although in many species the horns are reduced in length compared with the body of the uterus, but in the higher primates (Anthropoidea) the horns of the uterus fuse together during embryonic development to produce a unicornuate uterus composed of a single chamber. This is clearly an adaptation for producing single offspring, as is the reduction in the number of mammae to the single pair found in all higher primates and in many, though by no means all, prosimians. It is of interest that, even in women, the horns of the uterus may occasionally fail to fuse thus producing the primitive condition of a bicornuate uterus. Similarly, accessory nipples are sometimes found along the primitive mammary line.

One of the most important of the functional changes which has occurred in the pattern of reproduction in the primates is the extension of the period of childhood and adolescence before sexual maturity is reached. Tree-shrews are sexually mature at about six months after birth, most other prosimians at about two years, monkeys of both the Old and the New Worlds at about four years (with the exception of marmosets, which are mature at about one year), anthropoid apes at eight to ten years, and man at sixteen to eighteen years. This progressive lengthening of the pre-mature stage of life during which the offspring is still dependent on maternal care is accompanied by an increase in the size and complexity of the brain and in the development of learned behaviour and intelligence. It is generally believed that the increase in the capacity for learning is dependent on the postponement of maturity since the brain is thereby given a longer time in which to develop. Furthermore, it is likely that the postponement of maturity has been made possible by the reduction in litter size. There are two reasons why this should be so. Firstly, the members of a large litter must achieve independence of their mother before the arrival of the next litter, whereas single offspring can continue to receive maternal care since the burden on the mother is less severe. Secondly, it has been pointed out by Harrison, Weiner, Tanner and Barnicot (1964) that in multiple pregnancy the offspring are in competition with each other both before and after birth, so that rapidly developing individuals will be at an advantage over more slowly developing ones; when only one offspring is born this source of selection for rapid development will be eliminated. Empirical confirmation is provided by the marmosets, which regularly produce twins and which reach maturity much more rapidly than other monkeys.

Natural selection in Man

It has been assumed as a working hypothesis that the litter size typical of a species tends to evolve through natural selection towards an optimal size which leads on the average to the largest number of surviving offspring. We would therefore expect to find in those primates which usually have one baby at a time that the mortality in twins is so great that on average there are fewer survivors from a pair of twins than from one singleton. This is certainly not the case in man today. It will be seen from Table 3.4 on p. 54 that the combined stillbirth and infant mortality rate in England and Wales in recent years is about five per cent in single births, seventeen per cent in twins, and thirty-eight per cent in triplets; the average number of survivors per pregancy is therefore about 0·95 for single births, 1·66 for twins, and 1·86 for triplets, so that mothers of twins and triplets are at a selective advantage over mothers of singletons. It must be remembered, however, that infant mortality has been dramatically reduced in the course of the past century whereas natural selection requires many centuries, if not millennia, in which to work. We must therefore consider the rather scanty evidence available about the comparative mortality of twins in past centuries.

Data on mortality in Dublin in the years 1757–84 were published in a communication to the Royal Society in 1786 by the Master of the Lying-in Hospital, J. Clarke. He found that the perinatal mortality (stillbirths and deaths before sixteen days) was twenty per cent in single births and thirty-nine per cent in twins, so that the average number of survivors per pregnancy was 0·80 for single births and 1·22 for twins. Information about mortality in the rest of the first year of life is not available, but there is little doubt that it would reduce the differential between the average number of survivors from single and twin births still further. In addition maternal mortality was increased from one per cent in single to four and a half per cent in twin pregnancies; the death of the mother is equivalent to the death of all her potential future children and thus exerts a severe selective pressure. It can be concluded that in eighteenth-century urban conditions in Europe there was probably little difference in selective value between the production of twins and singletons.

Prior to the eighteenth century the only data available were obtained from the genealogical records of the ruling families of Europe in the sixteenth and seventeenth centuries by Peller (1944). The detailed breakdown of mortality is shown in Table 8.2, from which it will be seen that almost the same number of children survived to adult life from a twin as from a single pregnancy. When it is remembered that these data relate to a privileged group and that we must also take into account the effect of differential maternal mortality, there can be little doubt that prior to the eighteenth century the mother of twins was at a selective disadvantage compared with the mother of a single child. If we were able to pursue our investigation back

Table 8.2. *Mortality in twin and single births in the ruling families of Europe in the sixteenth and seventeenth centuries* (Peller 1944)

	Single births	Twins
Births (still and live)	4511	108
Stillbirths	97	12
First-week deaths	336	30
Deaths in the rest of the first year	627	18
Deaths in the second to fifth years	348	12
Deaths in the sixth to fifteenth years	193	2
Survivors beyond fifteen years	2910	34
Survivors per hundred births	64·5	31·5
Survivors per hundred pregnancies	64·5	63

to even earlier times we should probably find this disadvantage to be quite severe. It has been stated by Scheinfeld (1968) that: 'The practice of killing one or both twins was widespread among primitive peoples as diverse as the Eskimos, the Ainus of Japan, Australian aborigines, numerous Africans, and various North and South American Indians. Usually this practice stemmed from the excessive difficulty of sustaining and rearing two infants at the same time, a particular burden for people engaged in a constant struggle for existence. Among the Eskimos, where tribes were continually on the move in search of food, it was also extremely difficult, if not impossible, for a mother to carry two infants on her back simultaneously'.

  If we accept the thesis that mothers of twins were at a selective disadvantage in primitive times we can explain in evolutionary terms why twins are only rarely produced, but it is puzzling that there should be considerable genetic variability in the tendency to produce dizygotic twins. We found in Chapter 6 that the inheritance of twinning can be approximately explained on the assumption of a completely recessive gene, t, with a gene frequency of about $\frac{1}{2}$ in Caucasoid populations, which leads to the production of dizygotic twins in about three per cent of pregnancies in mothers with the homozygous genotype, tt. If all twins died before adolescence, then tt women would on average produce 0·97 surviving offspring for each surviving offspring produced by other women; that is to say they would be at a selective disadvantage of three per cent, so that the genotype tt would be at a selective disadvantage of one and a half per cent in the whole population of men and women. On the other hand, if mortality were the same in twins and singletons or were so small that its effect could be ignored, then the genotype tt would be at a selective advantage of one and a half per cent. (The effect of maternal mortality has been ignored in the above analysis.) It therefore seems reasonable to suppose that under primitive conditions the genotype tt was at a selective disadvantage of about one per cent, whereas today it is at a similar selective advantage.

It is shown in books on population genetics (see, for example, Li 1955) that a recessive gene with a frequency q and with a selective advantage s will increase in frequency by about $sq^2(1-q)$ per generation; if the recessive genotype is at a disadvantage then s will be negative and the gene frequency will decrease. If we put $s = 0·01$, $q = \frac{1}{2}$, and allow about four generations per century, this means that under modern conditions when the recessive genotype is at an advantage we would expect the gene frequency to increase by 0·01 in two centuries, or by 0·1, that is to say from 0·5 to 0·6, in two millennia. It is clear that selection is very slow and that we should not expect any appreciable change in the gene frequency to have occurred from the decrease in mortality over the past two centuries. This prediction is borne out by the limited evidence available. The frequency of twinning in the ruling families of Europe in the sixteenth and seventeenth centuries can be calculated from Table 8.2 as 54/4565 = twelve per thousand, which is about the same as in Europe today (see Chapter 4). In Sweden, where reliable birth statistics are available since the middle of the eighteenth century, the total twinning rate was about fifteen per thousand from 1750 to 1920, but has fallen to about twelve per thousand since then (Eriksson 1964); the decrease in the past forty years is confined to the dizygotic twinning rate and seems to occur in other Scandinavian countries, even after standardization for maternal age (see Table 4.7 on p. 92), but its cause is obscure.

Natural selection, though slow, must nevertheless be effective if given long enough to act. Why then was the gene for twinning not eliminated in pre-historic times during which the production of twins must almost certainly have been a disadvantage? There are two possible answers. Firstly, it has been suggested that primitive men lived in small hunting communities which rarely interbred with one another. Under such conditions random fluctuations in gene frequency will occur which may be of greater importance than natural selection if the population size is small enough. The mathematical theory of genetic drift, as this phenomenon is known, has been extensively studied, in particular by Sewall Wright; the reader is referred to the books by Falconer (1960) and Li (1955) for further details. There is no doubt that if the effective size of the breeding group is less than about a hundred, and if migration between groups is infrequent, genetic drift can keep in existence a gene against which there is a selection pressure of the order of one per cent. There is a general feeling among human geneticists that genetic drift has not played an important part in human evolution, but in our present state of knowledge it seems desirable to preserve an open mind.

The second explanation for the preservation of the twinning gene is that the disadvantage of producing twins is counterbalanced by some other advantage. If the gene acts through altering hormonal balance, as seems quite likely, it is reasonable to suppose that it will produce other effects; for example, it has been suggested by Anderson (1956) that there is a correlation between the production of twins and height, though this work requires confirmation. It is not enough, however, to postulate that these other effects have converted the selective disadvantage of the *tt* genotype into a selective advantage since in this case we would expect the *T* gene to be eliminated through natural selection. In order to explain the occurrence of both alleles in appreciable frequencies we must suppose that the heterozygote, *Tt*, is at a selective advantage compared with either of the homozygotes, thus producing a balanced polymorphism; the reader is again referred to the books mentioned in the previous paragraph for a fuller discussion. Heterozygote advantage has been suggested as an explanation of many human polymorphisms, including the blood groups, but the only well-documented case is sickle-cell anaemia which is due to a recessive gene found in parts of Africa, Greece, and Sicily where malaria was recently endemic. The homozygote with two sickle-cell genes suffers from severe anaemia which usually leads to early death; the heterozygote with one sickle cell and one normal gene is apparently normal, but there is evidence that he possesses greater resistance to malaria than the normal homozygote with no sickle-cell genes. Thus the selective advantage of the heterozygote keeps the gene in existence at a stable equilibrium frequency even though in double dose it is lethal. It is tempting to suppose that dizygotic twinning may also be a balanced polymorphism due to heterozygote advantage, but at the moment there is no evidence to support this conjecture. Another possibility is that the intermediate twinning rate in Cancasoids may be due to a cross between a race with a high twinning rate, such as the negroes, and a race with a low twinning rate, such as the Mongoloids. A similar explanation has been put forward to account for the distribution of the Rhesus blood group frequencies.

Bibliography

ALBERT, A., RANDALL, R. V., SMITH, R. A., and JOHNSON, C. E. (1956). The urinary excretion of gonadotrophin as a function of age, in *Hormones and the ageing process* (edited by E. T. Engle and G. Pincus), 49–62. Academic Press, New York.

ALLEN, E., PRATT, J. P., NEWELL, Q. U., and BLAND, L. J. (1930). Human tubal ova, related early corpora lutea and uterine tubes, *Contr. Embryol.* **32**, 45–76.

ALLEN, G. (1960a). A differential method for estimation of type frequencies in triplets and quadruplets, *Am. J. hum. Genet.* **12**, 210–24.

——, (1960b). The M quadruplets: 1. Probability of uniovular origin judged from qualitative traits, *Acta Genet. med. Gemell.* **9**, 240–54.

——, and BAROFF, G. S. (1955). Mongoloid twins and their siblings, *Acta genet. statist. med.* **5**, 294–326.

——, and FIRSCHEIN, I. L. (1957). The mathematical relations among plural births, *Am. J. hum. Genet.* **9**, 181–90.

——, HARVALD, B., and SHIELDS, J. (1967). Measures of twin concordance, *Acta genet. statist. med.* **17**, 475–81.

——, and KALLMANN, F. J. (1955). Frequency and types of mental retardation in twins, *Am. J. hum. Genet.* **7**, 15–20.

ANDERSON, D., BILLINGHAM, R. E., LAMPKIN, G., and MEDAWAR, P. B. (1951). The use of skin-grafting to distinguish between monozygotic and dizygotic twins in cattle, *Heredity, Lond.* **5**, 379–97.

ANDERSON, W. J. R. (1956). Stillbirth and neonatal mortality in twin pregnancy, *J. Obstet. Gynaec. Br. Emp.* **63**, 205–15.

ANDREASSI, G. (1947). Problemi e considerazioni sulla gravidanza multipla, *Medicus, Vatican City* **3** (2), 41. (Quoted by Gedda, 1951.)

ARCHER, J. (1810). Facts illustrating a disease peculiar to the female children of negro slaves; and observations showing that a white woman by intercourse with a white man and a negro may conceive twins, one of which shall be white and the other a mulatto; and that, vice versa, a black woman by intercourse with a negro and a white man may conceive twins, one of which shall be a negro and the other a mulatto, *Med. Reposit., N.Y.* 1, 319–23.

AREY, L. B. (1922). Chorionic fusion and augmented twinning in the human tube, *Anat. Rec.* 23, 253–62.

ASDELL, S. A. (1964). *Patterns of mammalian reproduction*, 2nd edn. Constable, London.

ASHER, P., and SCHONELL, F. E. (1950). A survey of 400 cases of cerebral palsy in childhood, *Archs Dis. Childh.* 25, 360–79.

AUSTIN, C. R. (1961). *The mammalian egg*. Blackwell, Oxford.

BAILEY, N. T. J. (1961). *Introduction to the mathematical theory of genetic linkage*. Clarendon Press, Oxford.

BARR, A., and STEVENSON, A. C. (1961). Stillbirths and infant mortality in twins, *Ann. hum. Genet.* 25, 131–40.

BENDER, S. (1952). Twin pregnancy. A review of 472 cases, *J. Obstet. Gynaec. Br. Emp.* 59, 510–17.

BENIRSCHKE, K. (1961). Twin placenta in perinatal mortality, *N. Y. St. J. Med.* 61, 1499–1508.

—— and DRISCOLL, S. G. (1967). The pathology of the human placenta, in *Handbuch der speziellen pathologischen Anatomie und Histologie* (edited by F. Henke and O. Lubarsch), 7 (5) (*Placenta*), 97–616. Springer-Verlag, Berlin.

BERG, J. M., and KIRMAN, B. H. (1960). The mentally defective twin, *Lancet* 1, 1911–16.

BERTILLON, M. (1874). Des combinasions de sexe dans les grossesses gémellaires (doubles ou triples), de leur cause et de leur caractère ethnique, *Bull. Soc. Anthrop. Paris.* 9, 267–90.

BOURNE, G. H. (1962). *The human amnion and chorion*. Lloyd-Luke, London.

BRAMBELL, F. W. R. (1956). Ovarian changes, in *Marshall's Physiology of reproduction*, 3rd edn. (edited by A. S. Parkes), 1 (1), 397–542. Longmans, London.

BRAND, D. J. (1963). Records of mammals bred in the national zoological gardens of South Africa during the period 1908 to 1960, *Proc. zool. Soc. Lond.* 140, 617–60.

BROWNE, F. J., and BROWNE, J. C. M. (1960). *Antenatal and postnatal care*, 9th edn. Churchill, London.

BUETTNER-JANUSCH, J. (1964). The breeding of galagos in captivity and some notes on their behaviour, *Folia primat.* 2, 93–110.

BULMER, M. G. (1958a). The numbers of human multiple births, *Ann. hum. Genet.* **22**, 158–64.

——, (1958b). A note on monozygotic twin diagnosis, *Ann. hum. Genet.* **22**, 340–1.

——, (1958c). The repeat frequency of twinning, *Ann. hum. Genet.* **23**, 31–5.

——, (1959a). The effect of parental age, parity and duration of marriage on the twinning rate, *Ann. hum. Genet.* **23**, 454–8.

——, (1959b). Twinning rate in Europe during the war, *Br. med. J.* **1**, 29–30.

—— (1960a). The familial incidence of twinning, *Ann. hum. Genet.* **24**, 1–3.

——, (1960b). The twinning rate in Europe and Africa, *Ann. hum. Genet.* **24**, 121–5.

BURROWS, H. (1949). *Biological actions of sex hormones*, 2nd edn. Cambridge University Press, London.

BURT, C. (1966). The genetic determination of differences in intelligence: a study of monozygotic twins reared together and apart, *Br. J. Psychol.* **57**, 137–53.

BUTLER, H. (1967). Seasonal breeding of the Senegal Galago (*Galago senegalensis senegalensis*) in the Nuba mountains, Republic of the Sudan, *Folia primat.* **5**, 165–75.

BUTLER, N. R., and ALBERMAN, E. D. (1969). *Perinatal problems.* (National Birthday Trust Fund.) Livingstone, Edinburgh.

——, and BONHAM, D. G. (1963). *Perinatal mortality.* (National Birthday Trust Fund.) Livingstone, Edinburgh.

BYRNS, R., and HEALY, J. (1936). The intelligence of twins, *J. genet. Psychol.* **49**, 474–8.

CARTER, C. O. (1962). *Human heredity.* Penguin Books, London.

——, (1965). The inheritance of common congenital malformations, *Prog. med. Genet.* **4**, 59–84.

——, and EVANS, K. A. (1961). Risk of parents who have had one child with Down's syndrome (mongolism) having another child similarly affected, *Lancet* **2**, 785–91.

CEDERLÖF, R., FRIBERG, L., JONSSON, E., and KAIJ, L. (1961). Studies on similarity diagnosis in twins with the aid of mailed questionnaires, *Acta genet. statist. med.* **11**, 338–62.

CHAPMAN, C. H. (1901). Observations on the placenta and young of *Dasypus sexcinctus*, *Proc. Acad. nat. Sci. Philad.* **53**, 366–9.

CHO, F. (1934). On twin pregnancy and birth, (In Japanese), *NipponFujinkag. Zasshi* **12**. (Cited in *Zentbl. Gynäk.* **59** (1935), 1741–2).

CLARKE, J. (1786). Observations on some causes of the excess of the mortality of males above that of females, *Phil. Trans. R. Soc.* **76**, 349–64.

COHRS, P. (1934). Eineiige Zwillinge bei Schaf und Schwein und zweieiige aber monofollikuläre Zwillinge beim Schaf, *Berl. tierärztl. Wschr.* **39**, 611–45.

CONVERSE, J. M., and DUCHET, G.(1947). Successful homologous skin grafting in war burn using identical twin as donor, *Plastic reconstr. Surg.* **2**, 342–4.

CORNER, G. W. (1955). The observed embryology of human single-ovum twins and other multiple births, *Am. J. Obstet. Gynec.* **70**, 933–51.

CORNEY, G., ROBSON, E. B., and STRONG, S. J. (1968). Twin zygosity and placentation, *Ann. hum. Genet.* **32**, 89–96.

COX, M. L. (1963). Incidence and aetiology of multiple births in Nigeria, *J. Obstet. Gynaec. Br. Commonw.* **70**, 878–84.

CURTIUS, F. (1928). Über erbliche Beziehungen zwischen eineiigen und zweieiigen Zwillingen und die Zwillingsvererbung im allgemeinen, *Z. KonstitLehre* **13**, 286–317.

DAHLBERG, G. (1952). Die Tendenz zu Zwillinsgeburten, *Acta Genet. med. Gemell.* **1**, 80–8.

DANFORTH, C. H. (1916). Is twinning hereditary?, *J. Hered.* **7**, 195–202.

DAVIS, E. A. (1941). *Linguistic skill in twins, singletons with siblings, and only children* (Inst. Child Welfare Mongr., Ser. 14). University of Minnesota Press, Minneapolis.

DAWES, G. S. (1968). *Foetal and neonatal physiology*. Year Book Medical Publishers, Chicago.

DAY, E. J. (1932). The development of language in twins: a comparison of twins and single children, *Child Dev.* **3**, 179–99, 298–316.

DE SIEBENTHAL, R. (1945). Les accouchements gémellaires à la Maternité de Genève de 1934 à 1943, *Mschr. Geburtsh. Gynäk.* **120**, 288–328.

DOYLE, G. A., PELLETIER, A., and BEKKER, J. (1967). Courtship, mating and parturition in the lesser bushbaby (*Galago senegalensis moholi*) under semi-natural conditions, *Folia primat.* **7**, 169–97.

DRILLIEN, C. M. (1964). *The growth and development of the prematurely born infant*. Livingstone, Edinburgh.

—— , (1968). Causes of handicap in the low-weight infant. In *Aspects of prematurity and dysmaturity* (Nutricia Symposium, edited by J. H. P. Jonxis, H. K. A. Visser, and J. A. Troelstra.) Stenfert Kroese, Leiden.

DUNCAN, J. M. (1865a). On some laws of the production of twins, *Edinb. med. J.* **10**, 767–81.

DUNCAN, J. M. (1865b). On the comparative frequency of twin-bearing in different pregnancies, *Edinb. med. J.* **10**, 928–9.

EASTMAN, N. J., and HELLMANN, L. M. (1966). *Williams Obstetrics*, 13th edn. Appleton-Century-Crofts, New York.

EDWARDS, J. H., and CAMERON, A. H. (1967). (Quoted by Strong and Corney 1967.)

ERIKSSON, A. W. (1964). Pituitary gonadotrophin and dizygotic twinning, *Lancet* **2**, 1298–9.

——, and FELLMAN, J. (1967). Twinning in relation to the marital status of the mother, *Acta genet. statist. med.* **17**, 385–98.

ESSEN-MÖLLER, E. (1941). Empirische Ähnlichkeitsdiagnose bei Zwillingen, *Hereditas* **27**, 1–50.

FALCONER, D. S. (1960). *Introduction to quantitative genetics.* Oliver and Boyd, Edinburgh.

——, (1965). The inheritance of liability to certain diseases, estimated from the incidence among relatives, *Ann. hum. Genet.* **29**, 51–76.

——, (1967). The inheritance of liability to diseases with variable age of onset, with particular reference to diabetes mellitus, *Ann. hum. Genet.* **31**, 1–20.

FERNANDEZ, M. (1915). Über einige Entwickelungsstadien des Paludo (*Dasypus villosus*) und ihre Beziehung zum Problem der spezifischen Polyembryonie des Genus Tatusia, *Anat. Anz.* **48**, 305–27.

FISHER, R. A. (1918). The correlation between relatives on the supposition of Mendelian inheritance, *Trans. R. Soc. Edinb.* **52**, 399–433.

——, (1919) The genesis of twins, *Genetics, Princeton* **4**, 489–99.

——, (1925). The resemblance of twins, a statistical examination of Lauterbach's measurements, *Genetics, Princeton* **10**, 569–79.

FRACCARO, M. (1956). A contribution to the study of birth weight based on an Italian sample, *Ann. hum. Genet.* **20**, 282–98.

——, (1957). A contribution to the study of birth weight based on an Italian sample: twin data, *Ann. hum. Genet.* **21**, 224–36.

FRANCOTTE, P. (1898). Recherches sur la maturation, la fécondation et la segmentation chez les Polyclades, *Archs. Zool exp. gén.* **6**, 189–298.

FRIES, S. (1880). Über die Fortpflanzung von *Meles taxus*, *Zool. Anz.* **3**, 486–92.

GALTON, F. (1875). The history of twins as a criterion of the relative powers of nature and nurture, *Jl. R. anthrop. Inst.* **5**, 391–406.

GEDDA, L. (1951). *Studio dei gemelli.* Edizioni Orizzonte medico, Rome.

GEMZELL, C., and ROOS, P. (1966). Pregnancies following treatment with human gonadotropins, with special reference to the problem of multiple births, *Am J. Obstet. Gynec.* **94**, 490–6.

GOTTESMAN, I. I., and SHIELDS, J. (1966). Contributions of twin studies to perspectives on schizophrenia, *Prog. exp. Personality Res.* **3**, 1–84.

GREENSPAN, L., and DEAVER, G. G. (1953). Clinical approach to the etiology of cerebral palsy, *Archs phys. Med.* **34**, 478.

GREULICH, W. W. (1934). Heredity in human twinning, *Am. J. phys. Anthrop.* **19**, 391–431.

GRÜNEBERG, H. (1952). Genetical studies on the skeleton of the mouse. IV. Quasi-continuous variation, *J. Genet.* **51**, 95–114.

GUSTAFSON, T. (1946). Observations of enlarged polar bodies and oocytary twins in *Psammechinus miliaris* (Gmelin), *Ark. Zool.* **38A**, 1–10.

GUTTMACHER, A. F. (1939). An analysis of 573 cases of twin pregnancy. II. The hazards of pregnancy itself, *Am. J. Obstet. Gynec.* **38**, 277–88.

———, and KOHL, S. G. (1958). The fetus of multiple gestations, *Obstet. Gynec., N.Y.* **12**, 528–41.

HADDOW, A. J., and ELLICE, J. M. (1964). Studies on bushbabies (*Galago* sp.) with special reference to the epidemiology of yellow fever, *Trans. R. Soc. trop. Med. Hyg.* **58**, 521–38.

HAMILTON, W. J., BROWN, D., and SPIERS, B. G. (1959). Another case of quadruplets, *J. Obstet. Gynaec. Br. Emp.* **66**, 409–12.

HAMLETT, G. W. D. (1932). The reproductive cycle in the armadillo, *Z. wiss. Zool.* **141**, 143–57.

———, (1933). Polyembryony in the armadillo: genetic or physiological?, *Q. Rev. Biol.* **8**, 348–58.

———, (1935). Delayed implantation and discontinuous development in the mammal, *Q. Rev. Biol.* **10**, 432–47.

HAMMOND, J. (1927). *The physiology of reproduction in the cow.* Cambridge University Press, London.

———, (1961). Fertility, in *Marshall's Physiology of reproduction*, 3rd edn. (edited by A. S. Parkes), **2**, 648–740. Longmans, London.

HANCOCK, J. (1954). Monozygotic twins in cattle, *Adv. Genet.* **6**, 141–81.

HANHART, E. (1960). 800 Fällen von Mongoloidismus in konstitutioneller Betrachtung, *Arch. Julius Klaus-Stift. Vererb. Forsch.* **35**, 1–312.

HANSON, E. (1960). *Cerebral palsy in Denmark.* Munksgaard, Copenhagen.

HARRISON, G. A., WEINER, J. S., TANNER, J. M., and BARNICOT, N. A. (1964). *Human biology.* Clarendon Press, Oxford.

HARRISON, R. J. (1963). A comparison of factors involved in delayed implantation in badgers and seals in Great Britain, in *Delayed Implantation* (edited by A. C. Enders), 99–114. University of Chicago Press, Chicago.

HARRISON, R. J., MATTHEWS, L. H., and ROBERTS, J. M. (1952). Reproduction in some Pinnipedia, *Trans. zool. Soc. Lond.* **27**, 437–540.

HARTMAN, C. G. (1932). Studies in the reproduction of the monkey *Macacus (Pithecus) rhesus*, with special reference to menstruation and pregnancy, *Contr. Embryol.* **23**, 1–162.

HAUGE, M., HERRLIN, K. M., and HEIKEN, A. (1967). The distribution of blood groups in a series of triplets, *Acta genet. statist. med.* **17**, 260–74.

HEADY, J. A., and HEASMAN, M. A. (1959). *Social and biological factors in infant mortalilty* (General Register Office, Studies on medical and population subjects, **15**). H.M. Stationery Office, London.

HELLIN, D. (1895). *Die Ursache der Multiparität der Unipaaren Tiere überhaupt und der Zwillingsschwangerschaft beim Menschen insbesondere.* Munich.

HENNING, W. L. (1937). A double sheep pregnancy with a single corpus luteum, *J. Hered.* **28**, 61–2.

——, (1939). Prenatal and postnatal sex ratio in sheep, *J. agric. Res.* **58**, 565–80.

HILL, A. B. (1966). *Principles of medical statistics*, 8th edn. Lancet, London.

HOLLISTER, N. (1924). East African mammals in the United States national museum, part III, *Smithsonian Inst. Bull.* **99**.

HOLT, S. B. (1955). Genetics of dermal ridges: frequency distribution of total finger ridge-count, *Ann. hum. Genet.* **20**, 159–70.

——, (1956). Genetics of dermal ridges: parent–child correlations for total finger ridge-count, *Ann. hum. Genet.* **20**, 270–81.

——, (1961a). Quantitative genetics of finger-print patterns, *Br. med. Bull.* **17**, 247–50.

——, (1961b). Inheritance of dermal ridge patterns, in *Recent advances in human genetics* (edited by L. S. Penrose), 101–19. Churchill, London.

HOLZINGER, K. J. (1929). The relative effect of nature and nurture on twin differences, *J. educ. Psychol.* **20**, 241–8.

HUNTER, J. (1787). An experiment to determine the effect of extirpating one ovarium upon the number of young produced, *Phil. Trans. R. Soc.* **77**, 233–9.

HUSÉN, T. (1953). Über die Begabung von Zwillingen, *Psychol. Beitr.* **1**, 137–45.

190   *Biology of Twinning in Man*

HUSEN, T. (1959). *Psychological twin research.* Almqvist & Wiksell, Stockholm. (Quoted by Scheinfeld, 1968.)

HYTTEN, F. E., and LEITCH, I. (1964). *The physiology of human pregnancy.* Blackwell, Oxford.

ILLINGWORTH, R. S., and WOODS, G. E. (1960). The incidence of twins in cerebral palsy and mental retardation, *Archs Dis. Childh.* **35**, 333–5.

JEFFREYS, M. D. W. (1953). Twin births among Africans, *S. Afr. J. Sci.* **50**, 89–93.

JENKINS, R. L. (1927). Twin and triplet birth ratios: the interrelations of the frequencies of plural births, *J. Hered.* **18**, 387–94.

——, and GWIN, J. (1940). Twin and triplet birth ratios: rigorous analysis of the interrelations of the frequencies of plural births, *J. Hered.* **31**, 243–8.

JOHANNSON, I., and HANSSON, A. (1943). The sex ratio and multiple births in sheep, *Lantbr-Högsk. Annlr.* **11**, 145–71.

JONES, F. W. (1915). The influence of the arboreal habit in the evolution of the reproductive system, *Lancet* **1**, 113–24.

——, (1916). *Arboreal man.* Arnold, London.

——, (1945). Some curiosities of mammalian reproduction. Part 3. Mammals that produce uniovular litters, *J. Obstet. Gynaec. Br. Emp.* **52**, 55–70.

JOUBERT, D. M., and HAMMOND, J. (1954). Maternal effect on birth weight in South Devon and Exeter cattle crosses, *Nature, Lond.* **174**, 647–8.

KALLMANN, F. J., and REISNER, D. (1943). Twin studies on the significance of genetic factors in tuberculosis, *Am. Rev. Tuberc.* **47**, 549–74.

KANG, Y. S., and CHO, W. K. (1962). The sex ratio at birth and other attributes of the newborn from maternity hospitals in Korea, *Hum. Biol.* **34**, 38–48.

KARN, M. N. (1952). Birth weight and length of gestation of twins, together with maternal age, parity and survival rate, *Ann. Eugen.* **16**, 365–77.

——, (1953). Twin data: a further study of birth weight, gestation time, maternal age, order of birth, and survival, *Ann. Eugen.* **17**, 233–48.

——, (1954). Data of twins born in Italy, 1935–51, *Acta Genet. med. Gemell.* **3**, 42.

——, LANG-BROWN, H., MACKENZIE, H., and PENROSE, L. S. (1951). Birth weight, gestation time and survival in sibs, *Ann. Eugen.* **15**, 306–22.

KARN, M. N., and PENROSE, L. S. (1951). Birth weight and gestation time in relation to maternal age, parity and infant survival, *Ann. Eugen.* **16**, 147–64.

KEAY, A. J. (1958). The significance of twins in mongolism in the light of new evidence, *J. ment. defic. Res.* **2**, 1–7.

KEMPTHORNE, O. (1955). The theoretical values of correlations between relatives in random mating populations, *Genetics, Princeton* **40**, 153–67.

——, and OSBORNE, R. H. (1961). The interpretation of twin data, *Am. J. hum. Genet.* **13**, 320–39.

KEYS, A., BROŽEK, J., HENSCHEL, A., MICKELSEN, O., and TAYLOR, H. L. *The biology of human starvation* (2 vols). University of Minnesota Press, Minneapolis.

KIRK, R. F., and CALLAGAN, D. A. (1960). Monoamniotic twin pregnancy, *Obstet. Gynec., N.Y.* **16**, 621–4.

KNOX, G., and MORLEY, D. (1960). Twinning in Yoruba women, *J. Obstet. Gynaec. Br. Commonw.* **67**, 981–4.

KOMAI, T., and FUKUOKA, G. (1936). Frequency of multiple births among the Japanese and related peoples, *Am. J. phys. Anthrop.* **21**, 433–47.

KÜPFER (1920). *Denkschr. schweiz. naturf. Ges.* **56**. (Quoted by Hammond 1927).

LACK, D. (1954). *The natural regulation of animal numbers.* Clarendon Press, Oxford.

——, (1966). *Population studies of birds.* Clarendon Press, Oxford.

LAWSON, J. B., and LISTER, U. G. (1955). *Clinical report of the Department of Obstetrics, University College, Ibadan, 1953–4.* Vail, London.

LE GROS CLARK, W. E. (1962). *The antecedents of man*, 2nd edn. Edinburgh University Press, Edinburgh.

LEITCH, I., HYTTEN, F. E., and BILLEWICZ, W. Z. (1959). The maternal and neonatal weights of some mammalia, *Proc. zool. Soc. Lond.* **133**, 11–28.

LI, C. C. (1955). *Population genetics.* University of Chicago Press, Chicago.

LIBRACH, S., and TERRIN, J. (1957). Monoamniotic twin pregnancy, *Am. J. Obstet. Gynec.* **74**, 440–3.

LILLIE, F. R. (1916). The theory of the free-martin, *Science, N.Y.* **43**, 611–13.

——, (1917). The free-martin: a study of the action of sex hormones in the foetal life of cattle, *J. exp. Zool.* **23**, 371–452.

LORAINE, J. A. (1963). Some clinical applications of assays of pituitary gonadotropins in human urine, in *Pituitary-ovarian endocrinology* (edited by R. I. Dorfman and M. Neves e Castro), 183–96. Holden-Day, San Francisco.

LOWTHER, F. DE L. (1940). A study of the activities of a pair of *Galago senegalensis moholi* in captivity, including the birth and postnatal development of twins, *Zoologica* **25**, 433–62.

MACARTHUR, J. W. (1938). Genetics of quintuplets. I. Diagnosis of the Dionne quintuplets as a monozygotic set, *J. Hered.* **29**, 323–9.

McDONALD, A. D. (1964). Monogolism in twins, *J. med. Genet.* **1**, 39–41.

MACDONALD, R. R. (1962). Management of second twin, *Br. med. J.* **1**, 518–22.

McKEOWN, T. (1961). Sources of variation in the incidence of malformations, in *First International Conference on congenital malformations* (edited by M. Fishbein), pp. 45–52. Lippincott, Philadelphia.

———, and RECORD, R. G. (1952). Observations on foetal growth in multiple pregnancy in man, *J. Endocr.* **8**, 386–401.

———, ———, (1953). The influence of placental size on foetal growth in man, with special reference to multiple pregnancy, *J. Endocr.* **9**, 418–26.

———, ———, (1954). Influence of pre-natal environment on correlation between birth weight and parental height, *Am. J. hum. Genet.* **6**, 457–63.

MALÉCOT, G. (1939). *Théorie mathématique de l'hérédité Mendelienne généralisée*, Guilhot, Paris. (Reprinted in Malécot, 1966.)

———, (1948). *Les mathématiques de l'hérédité*. Masson, Paris. (Reprinted in Malécot, 1966.)

———, (1966). *Probabilités et hérédité*, (Cahier 47 de l'Institut national d'études démographiques). Presses Universitaires de France, Paris.

MARSHALL, F. H. A. (1903). The oestrous cycle and the formation of the corpus luteum in the sheep, *Phil. Trans. R. Soc.* **196**, 47–98.

MARTIN, R. D. (1966). Tree-shews: unique reproductive mechanism of systematic importance, *Science, N. Y.* **152**, 1402–4.

MEDAWAR, P. B. (1957). *The uniqueness of the individual*. Methuen, London.

MEHROTRA, S. N., and MAXWELL, J. (1949). The intelligence of twins: a comparative study of eleven-year-old twins, *Pop. Stud.* **3**, 295–302.

MIJSBERG, W. A. (1957). Genetical-statistical data on the presence of secondary oocytary twins among non-identical twins, *Acta genet. statist. med.* **7**, 39–42.

MILLIS, J. (1959a). Distribution of birth weights of Chinese and

Indian infants born in Singapore: birth weight as an index of maturity, *Ann. hum. Genet.* **23**, 164–70.

MILLIS, J. (1959b). The frequency of twinning in poor Chinese in the maternity hospital, Singapore, *Ann. hum. Genet.* **23**, 171–4.

MONTAGU, M. A. F. (1962). *Prenatal influences*. Thomas, Springfield, Ill.

MORRIS, J. N., and HEADY, J. A. (1955). Social and biological factors in infant mortality, *Lancet* **1**, 343–9, 395–7, 445–8, 499–502, 554–9.

MORRIS, N., OSBORN, S. B., and WRIGHT, H. P. (1955). Effective circulation of the uterine wall in late pregnancy measured with ^{24}NaCl, *Lancet* **1**, 323–4.

MORTON, N. E. (1955). The inheritance of human birth weight, *Ann. hum. Genet.* **20**, 125–34.

——, CHUNG, C. S., and MI, M. (1967). *Genetics of interracial crosses in Hawaii* (Monographs in human genetics, **3**), Karger, Basel.

NAEYE, R. L. (1964). The fetal and neonatal development of twins, *Pediatrics, N.Y.* **33**, 546–53.

——, BENIRSCHKE, K., HAGSTROM, J. W. C., and MARCUS, C. C. (1966). Intrauterine growth of twins as estimated from liveborn birth-weight data, *Pediatrics, N.Y.* **37**, 409–16.

NAPIER, J. R., and NAPIER, P. H. (1967). *A handbook of living primates*. Academic Press, London.

NATIONAL BUREAU OF STANDARDS (1959). *Tables of the bivariate normal distribution function and related functions* (Applied Mathematics Series, **50**). U.S. Government Printing Office, Washington.

NEWMAN, H. H. (1917). *The biology of twins*. University of Chicago Press, Chicago.

——, (1923). *The physiology of twinning*. University of Chicago Press, Chicago.

——, FREEMAN, F. N., and HOLZINGER, K. J. (1937). *Twins: a study of heredity and environment*. University of Chicago Press, Chicago.

NICHOLSON, D. N., and KEAY, A. J. (1957). Mongolism in both of twins of opposite sex, *Archs Dis. Childh.* **32**, 325–7.

NISHIMURA, H., and SHIKATA, A. (1960). High embryonic mortality of the mouse fetuses from the elderly primigravid mothers, *Okajimas Folia anat. jap.* **36**, 151–4.

NISBET, J. (1953). Family environment and intelligence, *Eugen. Rev.* **45**, 31–40.

NYLANDER, P. P. S. (1969). The frequency of twinning in a rural community in Western Nigeria, *Ann. hum. Genet.* **33**, 41–4.

OSBORNE, R. H., and DE GEORGE, F. V. (1957). Selective survival in dizygotic twins in relation to the ABO blood groups, *Am. J. hum. Genet.* **9**, 321–30.

OWEN, D. B. (1962). *Handbook of statistical tables.* Addison-Wesley, Reading, Mass.

OWEN, R. D. (1945). Immunogenetic consequences of vascular anastomoses between bovine twins, *Science, N.Y.* **102**, 400–1.

PEARSON, K. (1931). *Tables for statisticians and biometricians,* Part 2. Biometric Laboratory, University College, London.

——, and LEE, A. (1903). On the laws of inheritance in man. I. Inheritance of physical characters, *Biometrika* **2**, 357–462.

PELLER, S. (1944). Studies on mortality since the Renaissance. D. Twins and singletons, *Bull. Hist. Med.* **16**, 362–81.

PENROSE, L. S. (1961). Genetics of growth and development of the foetus, in *Recent advances in human genetics* (edited by L. S. Penrose), 56–75. Churchill, London.

——, (1963). *The biology of mental defect,* 3rd edn. Sidgwick & Jackson, London.

PETTER-ROUSSEAUX, A. (1964). Reproductive physiology and behaviour of the Lemuroidea, in *Evolutionary and genetic biology of primates* (edited by J. Buettner-Janusch) **2**, 91–132. Academic Press, New York.

POTTER, E. L. (1961). *Pathology of the fetus and infant,* 2nd edn. Year Book Medical Publishers, Chicago.

——, (1963). Twin zygosity and placental form in relation to the outcome of pregnancy, *Am. J. Obstet. Gynec.* **87**, 566–77.

——, and CRUNDEN, A. B. (1941). Twin pregnancies in the service of the Chicago lying-in hospital, *Am. J. Obstet. Gynec.* **42**, 870–8.

——, and FULLER, H. (1949). Multiple pregnancies at the Chicago lying-in hospital, 1941–47, *Am. J. Obstet. Gynec.* **58**, 139–46.

PRICE, B. (1950). Primary biases in twin studies, *Am. J. hum. Genet.* **2**, 293–352.

RACE, R. R., and SANGER, R. (1954). *Blood groups in man,* 2nd edn. Blackwell, Oxford.

——, ——. (1962). ——, 4th edn.
——, ——. (1968). ——, 5th edn.

RAE, A. L. (1956). The genetics of the sheep, *Adv. Genet.* **8**, 189–265.

RAND, A. L. (1935). Habits of Madagascan mammals, *J. Mammal.* **16**, 89–104.

RAPHAEL, S. L. (1961). Monoamniotic twin pregnancy, *Am. J. Obstet. Gynec.* **81**, 323–30.

RAUSEN, A. R., SEKI, M., and STRAUSS, L. (1959). Twin transfusion syndrome. A review of 19 cases studied at one institution, *J. Pediat.* **66**, 613–28.

RECORD, R. G., GIBSON, J. R., and McKEOWN, T. (1952). Foetal and infant mortality in multiple pregnancy, *J. Obstet. Gynaec. Br. Emp.* **59**, 471–82.

RENKONEN, K. O. (1967). Is Weinberg's rule defective? *Ann. hum. Genet.* **30**, 277–80.

ROBERTS, D. F. (1964). Personal communication.

ROBSON, E. B. (1955). Birth weight in cousins, *Ann. hum. Genet.* **19**, 262–8.

ROGERS, B. O. (1963). Genetics of transplantation in humans, *Dis. nerv. Syst.* **24** (4) Pt 2, 7–43.

ROMER, A. S. (1959). *The vertebrate story*, 4th edn. University of Chicago Press, Chicago.

ROSS, W. F. (1952). Twin pregnancy in the African, *Br. med. J.* **2**, 1336–7.

RUSSELL, E. M. (1961). Cerebral palsied twins, *Archs Dis. Childh.* **36**, 328–36.

RYAN, R. R., and WISLOCKI, G. B. (1954). The birth of quadruplets with an account of the placentas and foetal membranes, *New Engl. J. Med.* **250**, 755–8.

SANDON, F. (1957). The relative numbers and abilities of some ten-year-old twins, *Jl. R. statist. Soc. A.* **120**, 440–50.

SANITER, R. (1901). Drillingsgeburten. Eineiige Drillinge, *Z. Geburtsh. Gynäk.* **46**, 347–84.

SCHEINFELD, A. (1968). *Twins and supertwins*. Chatto & Windus, London.

SCHIFF, VON F., and VERSCHUER, O. V. (1933). Serologische Untersuchungen an Zwillingen, *Z. Morph. Anthrop.* **32**, 244–9.

SHIELDS, J. (1954). Personality differences and neurotic traits in normal twin schoolchildren, *Eugen. Rev.* **45**, 213–46.

——, (1962). *Monozygotic twins, brought up apart and together*. Oxford University Press, London.

SIMMONS, R. T., GRAYDON, J. J., JAKOBOWICZ, R., and DOIG, R. K. (1960). A blood group genetical study made in a survey of illness in monozygotic and dizygotic twins, *Med. J. Aust.* **2**, 246–9.

SLATER, E., and SHIELDS, J. (1953). *Psychotic and neurotic illnesses in twins* (Medical Research Council Special Report Series, **278**). H.M. Stationery Office, London.

SMITH, A. (1955). A note on mongolism in twins, *Br. J. prev. soc. Med.*, **9**, 212–13.

SMITH, C. A. B. (1957). On the estimation of intra-class correlation, *Ann. hum. Genet.* **21**, 363–73.

SMITH, P. E. (1926). Ablation and transplantation of the hypophysis in the rat, *Anat. Rec.* **32**, 221.

SMITH, S. M., and PENROSE, L. S. (1955). Monozygotic and dizygotic twin diagnosis, *Ann. hum. Genet.* **19**, 273–89.

STEINER, F. (1935). Nachgeburtsbefund bei Mehrlingen und Ähnlichkeitsdiagnose, *Arch. Gynaek.* **159**, 509–23.

STERN, C. (1960). *Principles of human genetics.* 2nd edn. Freeman, San Francisco.

STEVENSON, A. C. (1959). Observations on the results of pregnancies in women resident in Belfast. III. Sex ratio with particular reference to nuclear sexing of chorionic villi of abortions, *Ann. hum. Genet.* **23**, 415–20.

——, (1960). The association of hydramnios with congenital malformations, in *Ciba Foundation Symposium on congenital malformations* (edited by G. E. W. Wolstenholme and C. M. O'Connor), 241–67. Churchill, London.

——, JOHNSTON, H. A., STEWART, M. I. P., and GOLDING, D. R. (1966). Congenital malformations. A report of a study of series of consecutive births in 24 centres, *Bull. Wld. Hlth Org.* **34**, supplement.

——, and WARNOCK, H. A. (1959). Observations on the results of pregnancies in women resident in Belfast. I. Data relating to all pregnancies ending in 1957, *Ann. hum. Genet.* **23**, 382–94.

STOCKARD, C. R. (1921). Developmental rate and structural expression: an experimental study of twins, 'double monsters' and single deformities, and the interaction among embryonic organs during their origin and development, *Am. J. Anat.* **28**, 115–277.

STORMONT, C., WEIR, W. C., and LANE, L. L. (1953). Erythrocyte mosaicism in a pair of sheep twins, *Science, N.Y.* **118**, 695–6.

STRONG, S. J., and CORNEY, G. (1967). *The placenta in twin pregnancy.* Pergamon, Oxford.

STURKIE, P. D. (1946). The production of twins in *Gallus domesticus*, *J. exp. Zool.* **101**, 51–63.

SUTTON, H. E. (1958). Selective survival in dizygotic twins, *Am. J. hum. Genet.* **10**, 233–4.

——, CLARK, P. J., and SCHULL, W. J. (1955). The use of multiallele genetic characters in the diagnosis of twin zygosity, *Am. J. hum. Genet.* **7**, 180–8.

SWYER, G. I. M. (1954). *Reproduction and sex.* Routledge & Kegan Paul, London.

TABAH, L., and SUTTER, J. (1954). Le niveau intellectuel des enfants d'une même famille, *Ann. hum. Genet.* **19**, 120–50.

TANNER, J. M. (1962). *Growth at adolescence*, 2nd edn. Blackwell, Oxford.

THORNDIKE, E. L. (1905). Measurements of twins, *Archs Phil. Psychol. scient. Meth.* 1, 1–64.

TORGERSEN, J. (1950). Situs inversus, asymmetry, and twinning, *Am. J. hum. Genet.* 2, 361–70.

VACCARI, A. (1908). *Contributo clinico-statistico allo studio della gravidanza multipla.* Tip. Derosi., Turin. (Quoted by Gedda 1951.)

VALLOIS, H. V. (1949). La repartition des groupes sanguins en France: l'Ouest armorico-vendéen, *Arch. Julius Klaus-Stift. Vererb-Forsch.* 24, 508–16.

VAN WAGENEN, G., and NEWTON, W. H. (1943). Pregnancy in the monkey after removal of the fetus, *Surg. Gynec. Obstet.* 77, 539–43.

VERMELIN, H., and RIBON, M. (1949). (Quoted by Corner 1955.)

VOÛTE, P. A. (1935). Tweeling-onderzoek (diagnostiek en methodiek), *Maandschr. Kindergeneesk* 5, 202–14.

WALKER, J., and TURNBULL, E. P. P. (1955). The environment of the foetus in human multiple pregnancy, *Etud. neo-natal.* 4, 123–48.

WALSH, R. J., and KOOPTZOFF, O. (1955). A study of twins: blood groups and other data, *Aust. J. exp. Biol med. Sci.* 33, 189–98.

WALTON, A., and HAMMOND, J. (1938). The maternal effects on growth and conformation in Shire horse–Shetland pony crosses, *Proc. R. Soc. B,* 125, 311–35.

WATERHOUSE, J. A. H. (1950). Twinning in twin pedigrees, *Br. J. soc. Med.* 4, 197–216.

WEINBERG, W. (1901). Beiträge zur Physiologie und Pathologie der Mehrlingsgeburten beim Menschen, *Pflügers Arch. ges. Physiol.* 88, 346–430.

——, (1909). Die Anlage zur Mehrlingsgeburt beim Menschen und ihre Vererbung, *Arch. Rass.-u. GesBiol.* 6, 322–39, 470–82, 609–30.

——, (1928). Mathematische Grundlage der Probandenmethode, *Z. indukt. Abstamm-.u. VererbLehre* 48, 179–228.

WENNER, R. (1956). Les examens vasculaires des placentas gemellaires et le diagnostic des jumeaux homozygotes, *Bull. Soc. r. belge Gynéc. Obstet.* 26, 773.

WHARTON, B., EDWARDS, J. H., and CAMERON, A. H. (1968). Monoamniotic twins, *J. Obstet. Gynaec. Br. Commonw.* 75, 158–63.

WILLIAMS, J. W. (1926). Note on placentation in quadruplet and triplet pregnancy, *Bull. Johns Hopkins Hosp.* 39, 271–80.

WILSON, E. B. (1925). *The cell in development and heredity,* 3rd edn. Macmillan, New York.

WISLOCKI, G. B. (1939). Observations on twinning in marmosets, *Am. J. Anat.* 64, 445–84.

WYSHAK, G., and WHITE, C. (1963). Birth hazard of the second twin, *J. Am. med. Ass.* 186, 869–70.

WYSHAK, G., and WHITE, C. (1965). Genealogical study of human twinning, *Am. J. publ. Hlth* **55**, 1586–93.

YUE, S. (1955). Multiple births in cerebral palsy, *Am. J. phys. Med.* **34**, 335.

YULE, G. U. (1924). A mathematical theory of evolution, based on the conclusions of Dr. J. C. Willis, F.R.S., *Phil. Trans. R. Soc. B.* **213**, 21–87.

ZAZZO, R. (1960). *Les jumeaux, le couple et la personne.* (2 vols.) Presses Universitaires de France, Paris.

Author Index

Subject Index